basic
PROJECTS

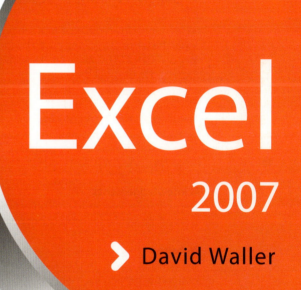

Excel
2007

> David Waller

www.payne-gallway.co.uk

✓ Free online support
✓ Useful weblinks
✓ 24 hour online ordering

01865 888070

PAYNE-GALLWAY

Payne-Gallway is an imprint of Pearson Education Limited, a company incorporated in England and Wales, having its registered office at Edinburgh Gate, Harlow, Essex, CM20 2JE. Registered company number: 872828

www.payne-gallway.co.uk

First published 2008

12 11 10
10 9 8 7 6 5 4 3

British Library Cataloguing in Publication Data
A catalogue record for this book is available from the British Library.

ISBN 978 1 905292 42 4

Designed by Wooden Ark Studios
Edited and Typeset by Sparks – www.sparkspublishing.com
Cover design by Wooden Ark Studios
Printed in China (SWTC/03)

Acknowledgements
Every effort has been made to contact copyright holders of material reproduced in this book. Any omissions will be rectified in subsequent printings if notice is given to the publishers.

Websites
The websites used in this book were correct and up-to-date at the time of publication. It is essential for tutors to preview each website before using it in class so as to ensure that the URL is still accurate, relevant and appropriate. We suggest that tutors bookmark useful websites and consider enabling students to access them through the school/college intranet.

Ordering Information
Payne-Gallway, FREEPOST (OF1771),
PO Box 381, Oxford OX2 8BR
Tel: 01865 888070
Fax: 01865 314029
Email: orders@payne-gallway.co.uk

CONTENTS

This book is all about using Excel. Excel is a program that allows you to create and use spreadsheets. A spreadsheet is a large grid in which you can enter text, numbers and, more importantly, **formulas** that carry out calculations using the numbers you have entered. One of the best things about using a spreadsheet program like Excel is that, if you change any of the numbers, then it will recalculate all of the formulas for you so you do not have to enter them all again.

This feature is very useful as it allows you to investigate what would happen *if* some of the numbers (data) were different. For example, if you create a spreadsheet to track your favourite football team and put in their points for each match played, you could see if they might win the league (or escape relegation) by adding points for their remaining unplayed matches. You can change these points and work out whether they need to win or draw or can afford to lose their unplayed matches. By doing this, you are carrying out what are called 'What if…' scenarios on the spreadsheet model you have created of your football team.

Spreadsheets are mainly used to work out finances, however. Companies use them to work out how much money they are earning – we call this **revenue** – and how much money they are making after they have paid out their costs – we call this **profit**, or **loss** if they are not making any money!

In the following tasks you will first learn some of the skills needed to use Excel and then you will be asked to make decisions about the kinds of text, numbers and formulas you will need to model a particular event and carry out 'What if…' scenarios. This will allow you to show your capability in using ICT and achieve higher National Curriculum levels.

The skills you will learn are:

Task 1: How to set up a spreadsheet and add text, numbers and formulas.
Task 2: How to add rows and columns and use Excel's inbuilt functions.
Task 3: How to create and format charts and graphs.
Task 4: How to use 'absolute' formulas and more advanced functions.

You are eventually going to create spreadsheets for a booking system for a school theatre production or concert. You will use it to work out the costs involved and how much money you will make by selling tickets, programmes and refreshments. You will be able to carry out 'what if…' scenarios by asking questions such as:

How much should the tickets cost to make a profit?

 How much money will we make if half of the people buy a programme?

 How many cups of tea and orange juice should we sell if we are to make a profit?

These screenshots show some of the features you will be using in Excel and the type of model you will be creating:

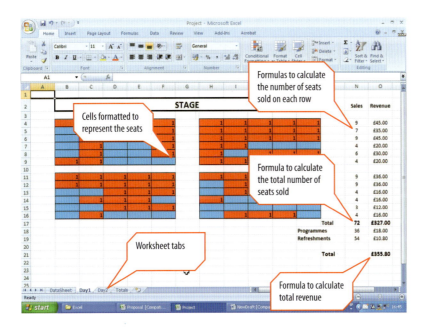

Figure Intro.1

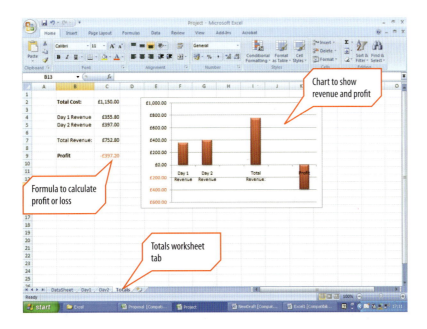

Figure Intro.2

Before we start with Task 1, though, the next few pages show you some of the most important skills that you'll need throughout your whole project: how to start the program, create new files and save your work. Remember you can return to these pages to remind yourself of these skills if you forget later on in the project.

This book also helps you to develop your Functional Skills in ICT. This is all about you being able to use your software skills in the way that best suits the activity that you have been given – in other words *why* you are doing something in the way that you have chosen. For example, you need to always be thinking about the purpose of what you are doing – what has it got to do with the project, what kind of impact do you want to achieve, who is going to see or use what you're working on i.e. who is your audience, and what is the background of the situation – for example, do you need to produce a formal or informal document? By considering all of these things you should be able to produce the right kind of documents that are 'fit for purpose', i.e. they do the job they need to do. A lot to take in at once I know, but have a look at the Functional Skills tabs as you work through the book and they'll show you what all this means in practice… so that you can use them to help you with your project.

SOFTWARE SKILLS
Selecting software program

FUNCTIONAL SKILLS
Choosing the best software to meet your needs means that your task will be completed in the most efficient and effective way – in these tasks we have chosen Excel because it is the best software package available to us for working with numbers and calculations

STARTING THE PROGRAM

Either

 Go to **Start** and **All Programs**.

 Select the **Microsoft Office** program group and then **Microsoft Office Excel 2007**.

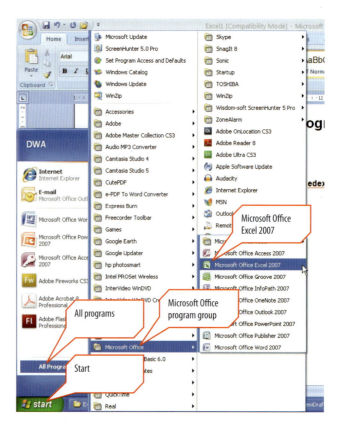

Figure Intro.3

Or

 3 Select the **Microsoft Office Excel 2007** shortcut on the desktop.

Figure Intro.4

CREATING A NEW FILE

 1 Click the **Office button**, at the top, left of the window.

Figure Intro.5

 2 Select **New** from the menu.

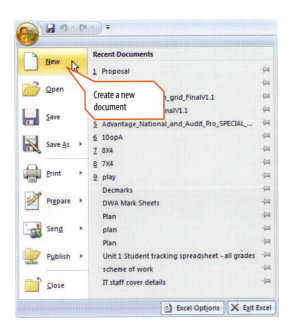

Figure Intro.6

Now double click **Blank Workbook**.

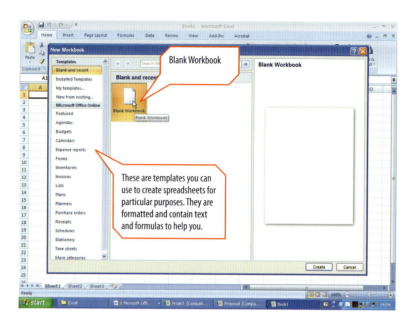

Figure Intro.7

 You will now see the Excel interface and all of the tools you will need to create spreadsheets.

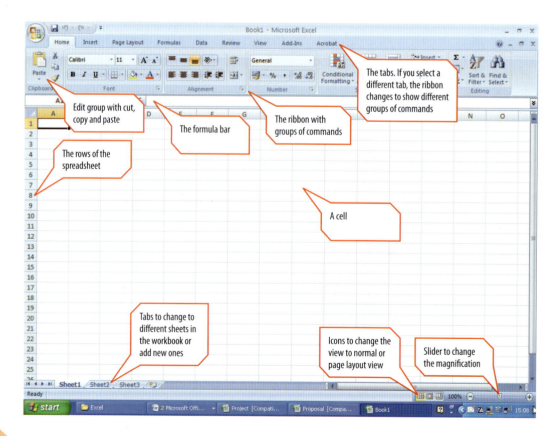

Figure Intro.8

SAVING A FILE

 Click the **Office button**, at the top, left of the window.

 Select **Save As** and you will see the options for saving the workbook.

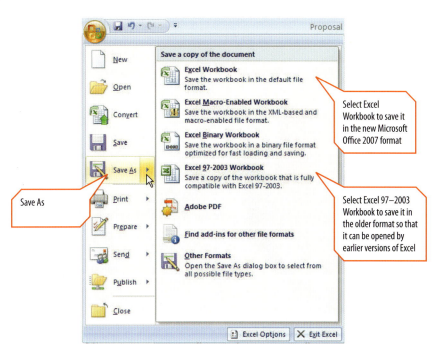

Figure Intro.9

 Now navigate to your home area and save the file in a suitable folder.

CREATING A SPREADSHEET TO MANAGE YOUR FINANCES

TASK BRIEF

You need to manage your own finances. It's time you started budgeting so that you can plan for all the things you will need to spend your money on each month and not run out!

Your friends are fed up with you always running out of money before the end of the month. You never have anything left for things like drinks and magazines, going to the cinema with them or buying them birthday and Christmas presents.

BRIEF

Your task is to create a spreadsheet model of your finances. You must use it to plan (budget) your money over the whole year. It must show how much money:

1. you have at the start of each month

2. you receive each month

3. you predict you will spend each month

4. you expect to have left at the end of the month.

As you create the spreadsheet model, you will cover the following:

SOFTWARE SKILLS

You will learn how to:

- Create a new spreadsheet
- Add text labels
- Fill a data series
- Add numbers
- Create formulas
- Copy formulas
- Format the cells

FUNCTIONAL SKILLS

As you work through this task the Functional Skills tabs will explain to you why the task tackles the brief in the way shown here and explain why you would choose to:

- Organise the layout of your spreadsheet
- Format the text and numbers
- Change the column width
- Use formulas
- Repeatedly fill cells with the same formula
- Change variables
- Test the spreadsheet

CAPABILITY

You will show that you can:

- Add or change simple formulas to develop a model
- Change variables to carry out 'What if...' scenarios

VOCABULARY

You should learn these new words and understand what they mean:

- Column
- Row
- Cell
- Formula
- Format
- Function
- Variable

RESOURCES

There is one file for this task that demonstrates what you will be creating in Excel:

Task1.xlsx

If you want to take a look at this file before you start you can download it from www.payne-gallway.co.uk

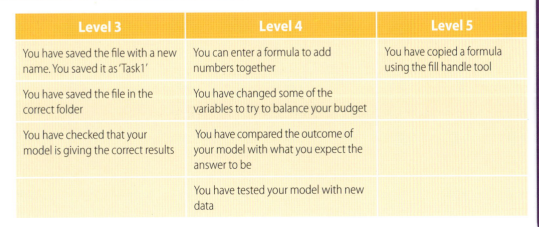

Level 3	Level 4	Level 5
You have saved the file with a new name. You saved it as 'Task1'	You can enter a formula to add numbers together	You have copied a formula using the fill handle tool
You have saved the file in the correct folder	You have changed some of the variables to try to balance your budget	
You have checked that your model is giving the correct results	You have compared the outcome of your model with what you expect the answer to be	
	You have tested your model with new data	

TARGET POINT

Have a look at the following statements before you start your task so you know what you are aiming for.

Although you will not be making your own decisions for much of this activity, these levels show you what you could be awarded when completing similar tasks on other work where you are working more independently and without following instructions.

OK. Let's get started.

Before you start any task, you should organise where you are going to save the work.

Create a folder called 'Excel' and inside it, create one called Task1 – this is where you will save the file you will be creating in this task.

SOFTWARE SKILLS
Creating a new file

FUNCTIONAL SKILLS
Organising your files and folder structure

STEP 1: CREATING THE SPREADSHEET AND THE LABELS

 Create a new file called **Task1** (see pages 7–9) and use **Save As** to save it in the Task1 folder.

When you create a new file you are starting a new **workbook** containing three worksheets (Sheet1, Sheet2 and Sheet3). You can move to different sheets by using the tabs at the bottom left of the window.

As you can see, in Figure 1.1, a worksheet is a very large grid made up of **columns** and **rows**. It looks just like a sheet you might use to play the game, battleships. So if you have played battleships before, then you will have no problem at all in learning how to use a spreadsheet!

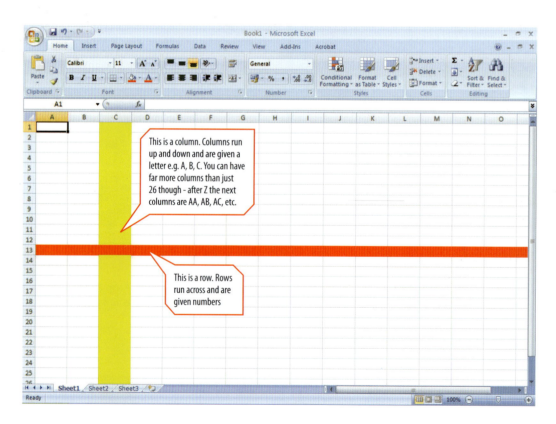

Figure 1.1

12

The boxes that are formed where a column meets a row are called **cells**. You can therefore use up to sixteen thousand million cells! Don't worry, we won't be using all of them in these tasks!

Every cell has an address, which is made up of its column letter and row number as shown in Figure 1.2. This figure shows the addresses of some of the cells. These are often referred to as **cell references**.

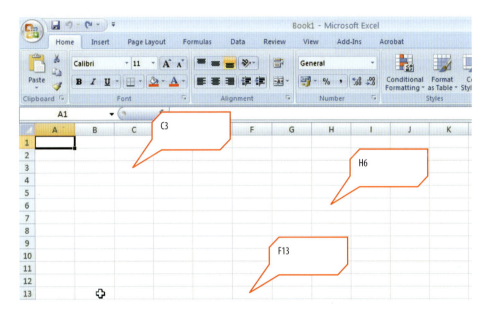

Figure 1.2

Text, numbers and formulas can be written in the cells but before we can do this they have to be made the **active cell** by clicking on them, as shown in Figure 1.3.

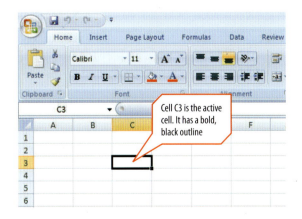

Figure 1.3

Above the worksheet is the ribbon, which has the **tabs** and **groups** of tools we will be using as we create the spreadsheet. We will learn to use these during the tasks.

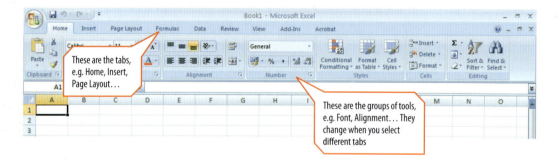

Figure 1.4

OK, that's the theory dealt with. If you understand about columns, rows and cells, then you can easily create a spreadsheet.

Adding text

 Every spreadsheet should have a title, so left click in cell A1 to make it the active cell and enter 'My Finance Planner' as shown in Figure 1.5.

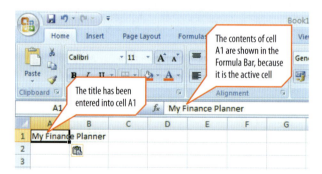

Figure 1.5

As you can see, the text spills out into column B. We will therefore make column A wider.

Changing column width

3 To make column A the exact width for the text, place the mouse pointer at the junction of the column A and column B headings and double click.

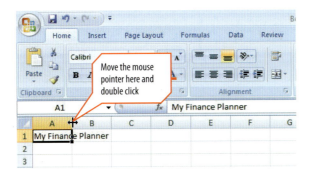

Figure 1.6

Column A will now be wide enough for the text.

Formatting text

4 Make sure that cell A1 is still the active cell as we will now format the text. Use the **Font** group of tools to change the font and background colours as shown in Figure 1.7. You'll find this group under the **Home** tab.

> **TIP**
>
> *Formatting means changing the appearance of data in a cell.*

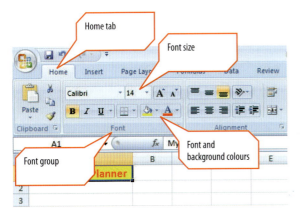

Figure 1.7

> **TIP**
>
> *You will have to resize column A again after you have changed the font size.*

We are now going to add the names of the months as column labels along row 2.

Using a series fill

 Enter 'January' into cell B2.

We could type in all of the months of the year but Excel has a very useful tool called **Series fill**. This is where Excel automatically fills in cells with a sequence of data, like the months of the year. You can create your own **series**, but Excel already knows the months of the year and the days of the week.

 Move the mouse pointer over the small box at the bottom-right corner of cell B2. It will turn into a small, black cross as shown in Figure 1.8.

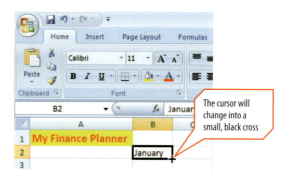

Figure 1.8

 Holding down the left mouse button, drag to the right. As you drag you will see the months that Excel will insert.

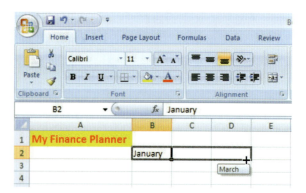

Figure 1.9

 When you reach December, release the left mouse button and the months will be inserted as shown in Figure 1.10.

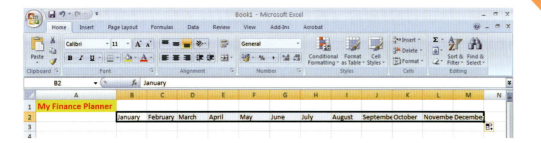

Figure 1.10

Changing text alignment

9   Now left click on the row 2 label to select the whole row and use the **Font** and **Alignment** groups of tools to make all of the month names bold and centred in their cells.

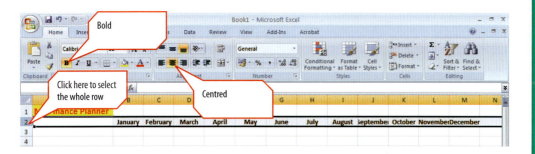

Figure 1.11

10   Now add the labels in column A, as shown in Figure 1.12.

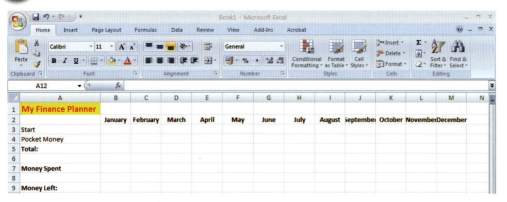

Figure 1.12

IMPORTANT TIP

When you make the font bold, you will have to resize the columns as you did in instruction 3 above.

Great – now we're ready to begin adding our data into the spreadsheet.

FUNCTIONAL SKILLS

Designing your spreadsheet layout – it's important to think about how you organise your information in your spreadsheet so that it's as easy to use as possible and it is set out in the way that allows you to perform your calculations easily. We have added a title, text labels above each column and at the start of each row so you know what the numbers that will be entered into the spreadsheet mean. The labels have been made bold so they stand out from the rest of the information, and the columns are wide enough to show all of the information in them

STEP 2: ADDING THE FORMULAS TO THE SPREADSHEET

When designing the formulas that are needed in the spreadsheet model, the first thing that we have to do is to work out what the **rules** of the model are.

In this example we are going to need three rules:

 A rule to work out how much money there is at the start of each month.

 A rule to work out the total money for each month.

 A rule to work out how much money is left at the end of each month.

Once we have worked out these rules, we can then convert them into formulas which we can enter into the spreadsheet.

SOFTWARE SKILLS
Creating rules

Creating rules

Let's work out the rules.

Rule 1:
The money at the start of each month is going to equal the amount left at the end of the previous month, e.g. the amount at the start of February will equal the amount left at the end of January.

Rule 2:
The total amount of money each month will equal the amount at the start plus the pocket money for that month.

Rule 3:
The money left at the end of each month will be equal to the total money for that month minus the money spent.

These are the rules of the spreadsheet model. Our next task is to convert these rules into formulas which will carry out these tasks. In a spreadsheet model you can add the formulas before there are any numbers to add up or take away.

 Make cell B5 the active cell. This is where the formula to carry out rule 2 is going to go.

This formula has to add the money at the start of January to the pocket money for January.

But we don't know which numbers have to be added up! That's OK because when we write the formulas we don't actually put the numbers in the formulas, we write in the cell references where the numbers can be found.

Creating formulas

In cell B5 we have to write a formula to add the number in cell B3 to the number in cell B4.

 2 In cell B5, therefore, write the following:

$$=B3+B4$$

The equal sign tells Excel that this is a formula and not just a piece of text.

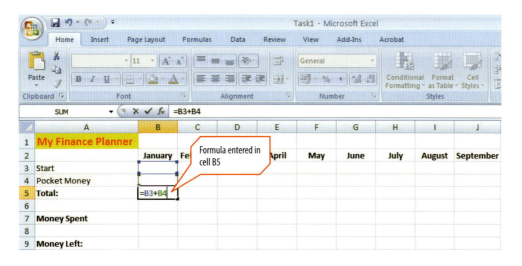

Figure 1.13

 3 To confirm the formula, either press the **Enter** key or click on the **tick** at the left of the formula bar.

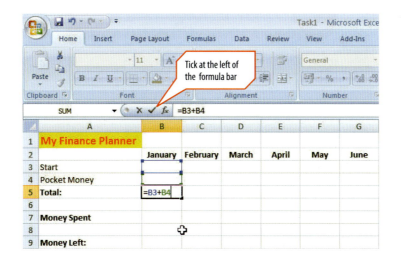

Figure 1.14

FUNCTIONAL SKILLS

Using formulas – creating a spreadsheet that uses formulas saves you a lot of time because it means that you can keep changing the numbers you use and the spreadsheet will automatically recalculate everything for you

The result of the formula will now be shown in cell B5, as shown in Figure 1.15.

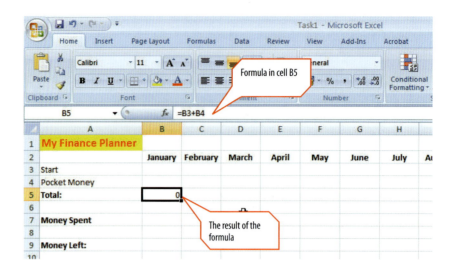

Figure 1.15

The formula has worked out that the number in cell B3 added to the number in cell B4 is equal to zero. That's because at the moment there are no numbers in these cells, but when you type some in the formula will recalculate and show the total.

Try this out but delete the numbers when you have finished!

IMPORTANT TIP

To delete the contents of a cell, click in the cell to make it active and press the Del key.

We now need similar formulas all along row 5 to find the total for each month in the year.

We could enter all of these in turn, so we could enter the formula:

=C3+C4

in cell C5 and carry on up to cell M5.

Fortunately we don't have to do this as Excel has **fill** capability. Remember how Excel 'filled' the cells with the months of the year? Well, here Excel will copy a formula into different cells and work out any changes that need to be made to the formula owing to it being in different cells.

Using the fill handle

4 Make sure that cell B5 is the active cell and move the mouse pointer over its **fill handle** – the small, black square in the bottom-right corner. (We used this when we filled the months of the year.)

When the pointer turns to a small, black cross, drag to the right to fill the cells with this formula up to column M, as shown in Figure 1.16.

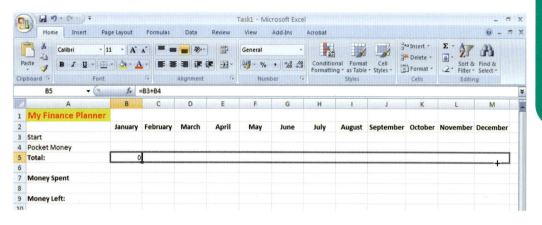

Figure 1.16

5 Release the left mouse button and you will see the results of the formulas as shown in Figure 1.17.

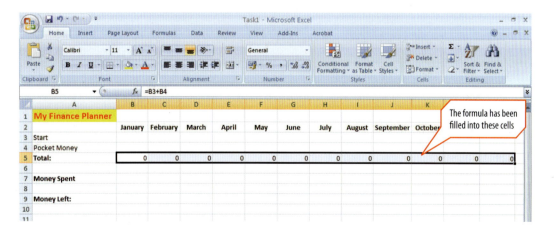

Figure 1.17

6 Click in cell C5 and check the formula.

Excel has changed the cell references as it has filled the formula along the row. It has changed =B3+B4 into =C3+C4.

Check all the way along that the formula has been changed to the correct cell references.

We can now add the formula for working out rule 3, to allow us to calculate the amount of money left at the end of each month. This will take the amount spent away from the total amount of money.

 7   We will enter the formula in a different way to the one we used in instruction 3.

> Make cell B9 the active cell and type in the equal sign to let Excel know that this is going to be a formula.

> Now left click in cell B5 and notice how this cell has been added to the formula in the formula bar.

> Now type in a minus sign.

> Left click in cell B7.

The formula should now be as shown in Figure 1.18.

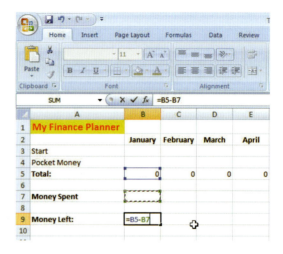

Figure 1.18

Set the formula by clicking on the tick or by pressing the **Enter** key.

 8   Now use the fill handle of cell B9 to fill the formula up to column M as shown in Figure 1.19.

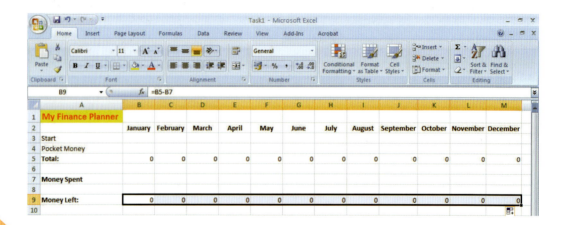

Figure 1.19

We can now enter the formula for rule 1, to calculate the amount of money at the start of each month. This is the easiest formula as it only has to copy the amount left at the end of the previous month.

We are going to assume that you spent all your money over Christmas and there isn't any at the start of the new year!

 9   Make cell C3 the active cell and enter the formula:

$$=B9$$

You can use either of the two methods: either type in the cell address or click on cell B9.

 10   Make sure cell C3 is the active cell again and use the fill handle to fill the formula along row 3 up to column M, as shown in Figure 1.20.

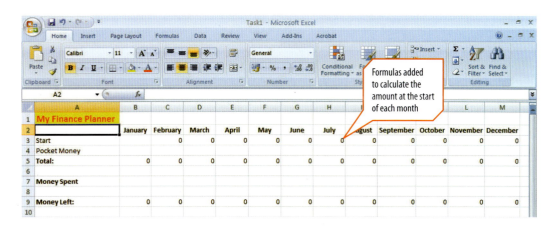

Figure 1.20

We have now added all of the formulas to ensure that all of the rules are carried out.

STEP 3: FORMATTING THE CELLS

When we entered the title of the spreadsheet model, we formatted cell A1 and changed the font and its size and the background colour. However you can also format the cells and change how they will display the numbers you enter or the calculated formulas.

In our model, all of the cells containing numbers need to be formatted for currency.

Setting the number format

 Click on the row number for row 3 to highlight the whole row as shown in Figure 1.21.

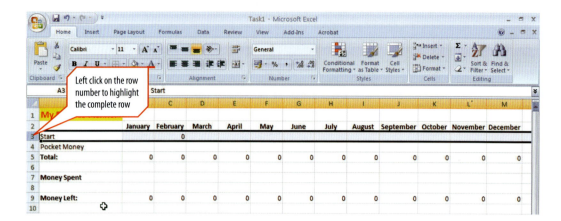

Figure 1.21

 Now holding down the **Ctrl** key, click on the row numbers of rows 4, 5, 7 and 9 so that all of these rows are highlighted.

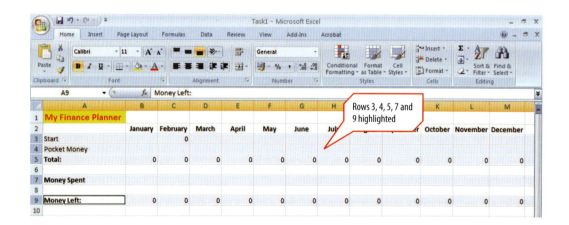

Figure 1.22

3 Now use the **Number** group of tools in the centre of the ribbon.

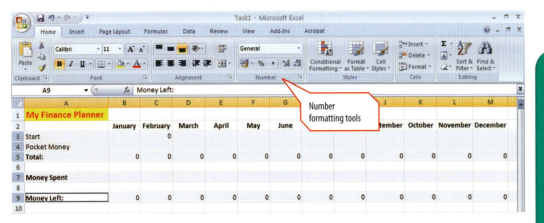

Figure 1.23

 4 Click on the arrow to see the alternative ways of formatting the cells and select **Currency**.

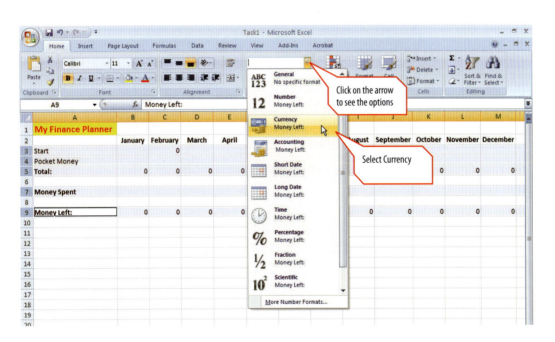

Figure 1.24

The cells should now all be formatted for currency.

We are now going to set the format for showing negative numbers so that the model can show us if we're planning to spend too much.

Click on the small arrow at the bottom-right corner of the **Number** group of tools.

Figure 1.25

You will now see the **Format Cells** dialogue box. As the rows are still selected the currency option is selected in the dialogue box.

 Select the fourth option for displaying negative numbers, which is with a minus sign and in a red font.

You might have heard the phrase 'going into the red' – it just means spending more money than you have.

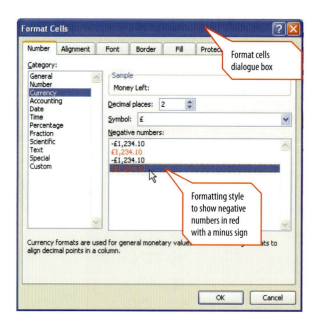

Figure 1.26

All of the formatting is now complete but before we start to add data to our model we need to test it.

STEP 4: TESTING THE MODEL

Before we start using the model to plan a budget we should test it to ensure that we have not made any errors with the rules and the formulas. Never accept the results from a spreadsheet until you have tested it with the best computer in the world – your brain!

Test data:

January pocket money: £10

January money spent: £11

If the rules and formulas are correct then the money left at the end of January should be £1.00, and it should have a minus sign and be in a red font.

The amount at the start of each month, which is the total for the month plus the amount left from the previous month, should therefore be –£1.00 for all months because we haven't added any more money to any of the months.

 Enter the test data. The spreadsheet should be like that shown in Figure 1.27.

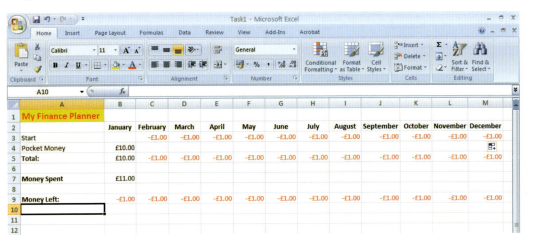

	A	B	C	D	E	F	G	H	I	J	K	L	M
1	My Finance Planner												
2		January	February	March	April	May	June	July	August	September	October	November	December
3	Start		–£1.00	–£1.00	–£1.00	–£1.00	–£1.00	–£1.00	–£1.00	–£1.00	–£1.00	–£1.00	–£1.00
4	Pocket Money	£10.00											
5	Total:	£10.00	–£1.00	–£1.00	–£1.00	–£1.00	–£1.00	–£1.00	–£1.00	–£1.00	–£1.00	–£1.00	–£1.00
6													
7	Money Spent	£11.00											
8													
9	Money Left:	–£1.00	–£1.00	–£1.00	–£1.00	–£1.00	–£1.00	–£1.00	–£1.00	–£1.00	–£1.00	–£1.00	–£1.00
10													
11													
12													

Figure 1.27

 Well done! All the formulas are correct so delete all of the test data from B4 and B7 and we will start to use the model to plan our budget for the year.

IMPORTANT WARNING

When deleting the data be careful not to delete any of the formulas. Just delete the numbers you have typed in.

STEP 5: USING THE MODEL

We can now start to use the model to plan our budget for the coming year.

 Enter the pocket money for each month (you could call this your **income**). Remember to make life easy for yourself and use Excel to help you to copy data from one cell to another.

We will assume that this will be £10 each month so enter this in row 4 as shown in Figure 1.28.

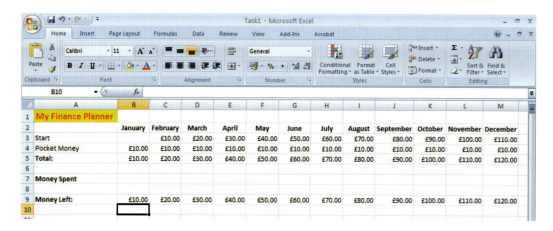

The spreadsheet shows "My Finance Planner":

	A	January	February	March	April	May	June	July	August	September	October	November	December
3	Start		£10.00	£20.00	£30.00	£40.00	£50.00	£60.00	£70.00	£80.00	£90.00	£100.00	£110.00
4	Pocket Money	£10.00	£10.00	£10.00	£10.00	£10.00	£10.00	£10.00	£10.00	£10.00	£10.00	£10.00	£10.00
5	Total:	£10.00	£20.00	£30.00	£40.00	£50.00	£60.00	£70.00	£80.00	£90.00	£100.00	£110.00	£120.00
6													
7	Money Spent												
8													
9	Money Left:	£10.00	£20.00	£30.00	£40.00	£50.00	£60.00	£70.00	£80.00	£90.00	£100.00	£110.00	£120.00

Figure 1.28

2 We can now enter the amounts you know that we will need at certain times during the year, such as for summer holidays, and birthday and Christmas presents.

> March: £10 for a birthday present.

> May: £10 for a birthday present.

> August: £50 for the holidays.

> December: £30 for Christmas presents.

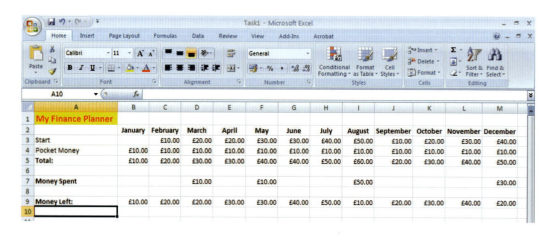

The spreadsheet shows "My Finance Planner":

	A	January	February	March	April	May	June	July	August	September	October	November	December
3	Start		£10.00	£20.00	£20.00	£30.00	£30.00	£40.00	£50.00	£10.00	£20.00	£30.00	£40.00
4	Pocket Money	£10.00	£10.00	£10.00	£10.00	£10.00	£10.00	£10.00	£10.00	£10.00	£10.00	£10.00	£10.00
5	Total:	£10.00	£20.00	£30.00	£30.00	£40.00	£40.00	£50.00	£60.00	£20.00	£30.00	£40.00	£50.00
6													
7	Money Spent			£10.00		£10.00			£50.00				£30.00
8													
9	Money Left:	£10.00	£20.00	£20.00	£30.00	£30.00	£40.00	£50.00	£10.00	£20.00	£30.00	£40.00	£20.00

Figure 1.29

Changing variables in the spreadsheet

3 You can now add the amounts you can afford to spend on the cinema, drinks, magazines, etc., during the year. You can experiment with different amounts but you must never go into the red!

This means you will have to change the amounts you enter. These values that you enter and can change are called **variables**. Figure 1.30 shows an example.

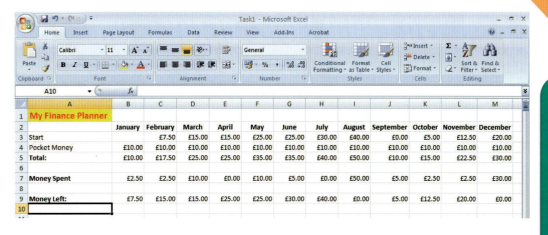

	A	B	C	D	E	F	G	H	I	J	K	L	M
1	My Finance Planner												
2		January	February	March	April	May	June	July	August	September	October	November	December
3	Start		£7.50	£15.00	£15.00	£25.00	£25.00	£30.00	£40.00	£0.00	£5.00	£12.50	£20.00
4	Pocket Money	£10.00	£10.00	£10.00	£10.00	£10.00	£10.00	£10.00	£10.00	£10.00	£10.00	£10.00	£10.00
5	Total:	£10.00	£17.50	£25.00	£25.00	£35.00	£35.00	£40.00	£50.00	£10.00	£15.00	£22.50	£30.00
6													
7	Money Spent	£2.50	£2.50	£10.00	£0.00	£10.00	£5.00	£0.00	£50.00	£5.00	£2.50	£2.50	£30.00
8													
9	Money Left:	£7.50	£15.00	£15.00	£25.00	£25.00	£30.00	£40.00	£0.00	£5.00	£12.50	£20.00	£0.00
10													

Figure 1.30

You will have to make some tough decisions so you can balance your budget (make your money spent equal to or less than your income) and never go into the red. What will you cut back on?

CHECKPOINT

You should be able to:

- Explain the terms column, row, cell, formula.
- Create a new workbook.
- Use 'Save As' to save the worksheet in a specified folder.
- Add text labels.
- Format text including font, font size, font colour and background colour.
- Change the width of columns.
- Add formulas.
- Format numbers for currency.
- Test the spreadsheet.
- Use the spreadsheet to plan your budget.

ASSESSMENT POINT

Now let's assess the work. Look back at the table at the beginning of this section (**Target Point**) and decide on which of the statements you can answer 'Yes' to.

Did you do as well as you expected? Could you improve your work? Add a comment to your work to show what you could do to improve it so that next time you'll remember to do it the first time.

DEVELOPING YOUR SPREADSHEET TO SHOW MORE DETAILS AND ANALYSE THE DATA

TASK BRIEF

You need to improve your spreadsheet so that it allows you to show all the different ways in which you spend your money, or to add income from other sources such as gifts or a job.

The spreadsheet you created in Task 1 met all of the requirements in the task brief but we could make it better. We could also look at how to analyse the data and look at patterns like the number of months that you buy CDs or visit the cinema. For this we will look at using 'What if …' scenarios.

Your task here therefore is to improve the spreadsheet model of your finances. In addition to all of the requirements in Task 1 it must now allow you to:

1. show the different ways in which you spend your money (we'll call these costs)

2. allow you to enter income from other sources like a job

3. show the average, maximum and minimum amounts spent each month on different things such as magazines, CDs, music downloads or visits to the cinema

4. count up the number of months that you plan cinema visits or buy CDs.

As you create the spreadsheet model, you will cover the following:

SOFTWARE SKILLS

You will learn how to:

- Protect cells in a spreadsheet
- Add new rows to the spreadsheet
- Use the SUM function to find totals
- Use the AVERAGE, MAX and MIN functions
- Use the COUNTIF function
- Use conditional formatting

FUNCTIONAL SKILLS

As you work through this task the Functional Skills tabs will explain to you why the task tackles the brief in the way shown here and explain why you would choose to:

- Manage your files and folders
- Add data to your spreadsheet
- Use functions
- Use cell ranges

CAPABILITY

You will show that you can:

- Add or change formulas to develop a model
- Use inbuilt functions, such as SUM, COUNTIF, AVERAGE, MAX and MIN
- Change variables to carry out 'What if...' scenarios

VOCABULARY

You should learn these new words and understand what they mean.

- Function
- Average
- Maximum
- Minimum
- CountIf

RESOURCES

There is one file for this task that demonstrates what you will be creating in Excel:

Task2.xlsx

If you want to take a look at this file before you start you can download it from www.payne-gallway.co.uk

Level 3	Level 4	Level 5	Level 6
You have saved the file with a new name. You saved it as 'Task2'	You can enter a formula to add numbers together	You have copied a formula using the fill handle tool	You have used the COUNTIF function in your spreadsheet
You have saved the file in the correct folder	You have saved the file with a new name in a new folder	You have used the SUM, MAX and MIN functions in your spreadsheet	
You have checked that your model is giving the correct results	You have added the data to your model outlined in the task brief	You have used conditional formatting to look for patterns in the data	
	You have changed some of the variables to try to balance your budget		

 **TARGET POINT**

Have a look at the following statements before you start your task so you know what you are aiming for.

Although you will not be making your own decisions for much of this activity, these levels show you what you could be awarded when completing similar tasks on other work where you are working more independently and without following instructions.

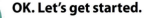

Before you start any task, you should organise your area where you are going to save the work.

 Create a new folder inside the 'Excel' folder and name it Task2 – this is where you will save the file you will be creating in this task.

 Open the Task1 worksheet and use 'Save As' to save it in the Task2 folder, calling it **Task2**.

STEP 1: PROTECTING THE SPREADSHEET AND ADDING ROWS AND FUNCTIONS

We are going to make the model more realistic by adding extra information about your income and costs. We will therefore need to add new rows in which to enter this data but before we do that we will delete the data we have already entered into the sheet. We don't want to delete the formulas we entered, only the variables – the pocket money and the money spent. We will therefore lock the cells containing the formulas.

> **TIP**
>
> *Actually, when you 'protect' a worksheet, all of the cells become locked so in fact we don't have to lock the cells containing the formulas, we have to unlock the cells containing the variables.*

Protecting cells

 Highlight the whole of row 4 by clicking on the row number and then select **Format** in the **Cells** group of tools. Select **Format Cells** at the bottom of the menu.

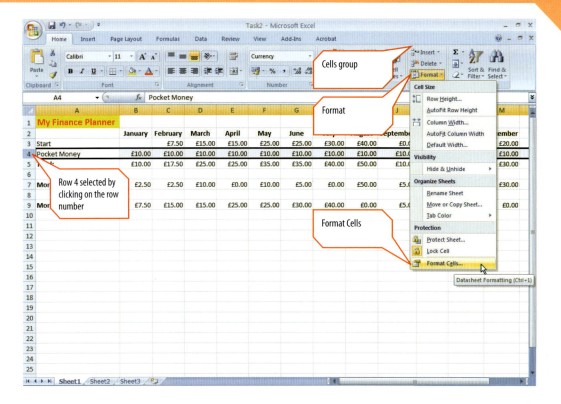

Figure 2.1

2 Select the **Protection** tab and then click in the **Locked** box to remove the green tick and then click on **OK**.

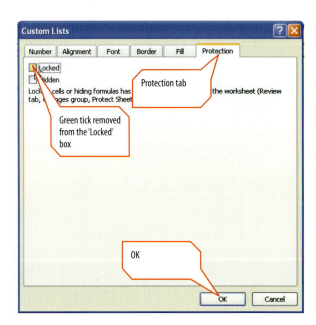

Figure 2.2

3 Do the same procedure to unlock the cells in row 7.

Now select **Protect Sheet** from the drop-down **Format** menu in the **Cells** group.

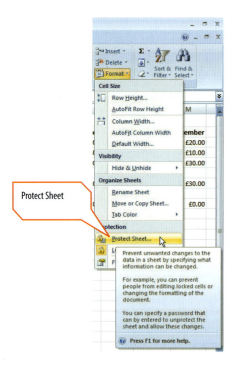

Figure 2.3

 You could set a password that would have to be used by anyone who tried to unprotect the sheet, but in this case just leave it blank and click on **OK**.

Figure 2.4

6 You can now select the cells containing the pocket money and money spent variables and press the **Del** key to delete them.

If you try to delete the formulas or text from any of the other cells, you will see the error message shown in Figure 2.5.

Figure 2.5

Unprotecting a sheet

As we now need to add new data and rows we'll have to unprotect the sheet again.

7 So now select **Unprotect Sheet** from the drop-down **Format** menu in the **Cells** group.

Figure 2.6

Adding rows

We now need to add some more rows for the extra data we need to add. As you would expect, there are several ways to do this.

 Click in cell A5 to make it the active cell and then select **Insert** in the **Cells** group.

Select **Insert Sheet Rows** as shown in Figure 2.7.

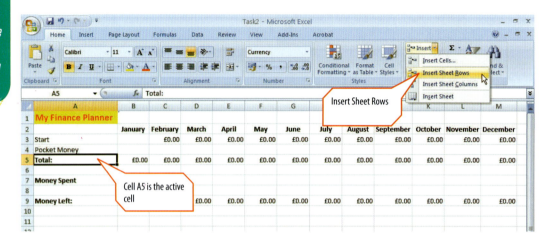

Figure 2.7

A row will be inserted above the row with the active cell. You can format it like the rows above or below, as shown in Figure 2.8.

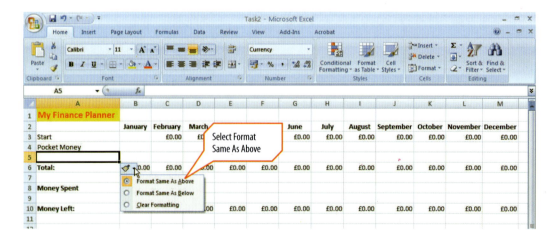

Figure 2.8

We'll add another row using another method.

9 Right click in cell A5 and select **Insert** from the menu.

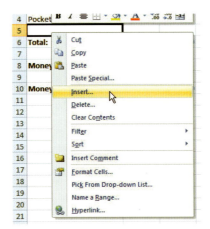

Figure 2.9

 10 Now select **Entire Row** from the menu and then click on **OK**.

Figure 2.10

 11 Add rows and text labels in column A as shown in Figure 2.11.

Figure 2.11

We have now included new rows for adding more details about our income and costs, but the formulas in rows 8 and 19 are incorrect because they don't include the new rows we have added. We will have to change them.

Deleting data in a sheet

 Highlight the cells in rows 8 and 19 from column B to column M and press the **Del** key to delete the contents of the cells so that the spreadsheet looks like that in Figure 2.12.

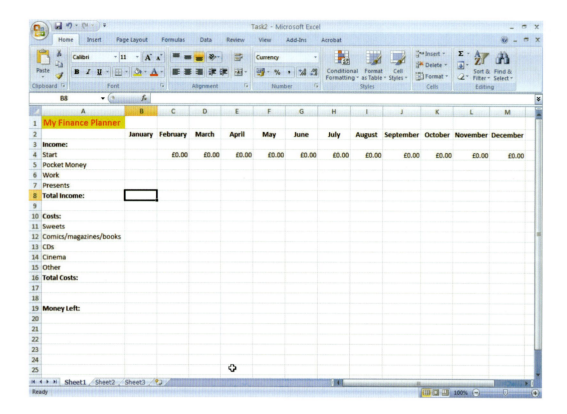

Figure 2.12

We will now insert functions to find the totals for the income and the costs.

 Make cell B8 the active cell and select the **Formulas** tab.

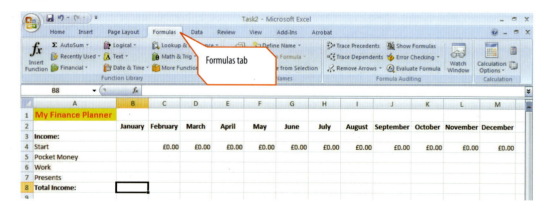

Figure 2.13

Using the SUM function

 14 Now select the **Autosum** function – this finds the total of all the numbers between two cells (the start and the end cell of the row or column you are finding the total of).

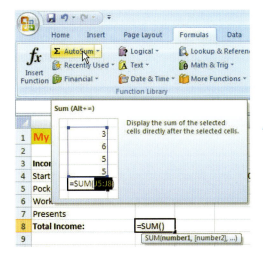

Figure 2.14

The function has been inserted into cell B8. You must now insert the first and last cell reference of the column you are adding up.

 15 Left click in cell B4 and drag down to cell B7 to insert the start and end cells as shown in Figure 2.15. Then click the tick icon to the left of the formula bar or press the **Enter** key.

Figure 2.15

FUNCTIONAL SKILLS

Using functions – functions make it easier to work out what your formulas need to be because you don't need to remember the mathematical calculation, just what you want to do with the numbers, e.g. work out the average, the total, the maximum, the minimum...

Using cell ranges – cell ranges make it quicker to work out the results for a large column or row of numbers because it means you don't have to type in each cell reference

 16 Now use the fill handle of cell B8 to fill the function along row 8 up to column M.

17 Now add the autosum function to cell B16 with B11 and B15 as the start and end cells.

Use the fill handle of cell B16 to fill the function along row 16 up to column M.

That works out our total income and costs but now we want to work out the money we have left at the end of each month, i.e. total income – total costs.

 18 Make B18 the active cell and enter the following formula to calculate the amount left at the end of the month:

=B8-B16

 19 Use the fill handle to fill this formula along the row to column M.

The spreadsheet should now be like Figure 2.16.

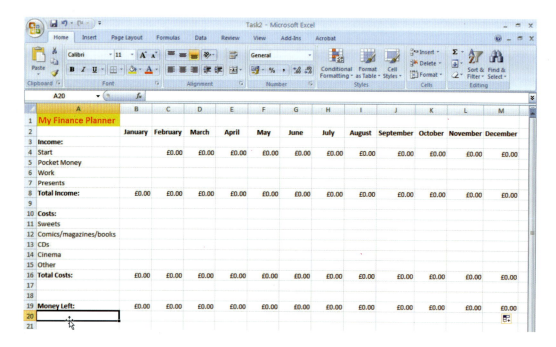

Figure 2.16

Great – you have now created the formulas which will:

> add up all of your income (including that from the new sources we have added)

> add up all of your costs

> work out the money you have left at the end of each month.

STEP 2: TESTING THE SPREADSHEET

Before you use your spreadsheet with real data, it's always a good idea to check it first and make sure that the formulas do what you want them to! Let's now test the spreadsheet to check that the formulas are correct.

 Enter the following amounts for January:

> Pocket Money: £10.00

> Work: £15.00

> Presents: £0.00

> Sweets: £5.00

> Comics/Magazines   £2.50

> CDs   £0.00

> Cinema   £5.00

> Other   £3.00

If the formulas are correct the totals should be:

> Total Income   £25.00

> Total Costs   £15.50

> Money Left   £9.50

> Start of February   £9.50

Well done! All the functions and formulas are working correctly.

STEP 3: ENTERING DATA TO CREATE THE BUDGET

Like you did in Task 1, you must now enter your plans for the year ahead. When you're creating a budget like this you will normally know what your income will be because it will be the same each month (except when you receive money as gifts), so you should enter it first. Then when you know your income you can work out what you have to spend and plan how to spend it. Remember, you cannot go into the red! For this task, though, use the data in the spreadsheet shown here. When you have entered it all your spreadsheet should look something like the one shown in Figure 2.17.

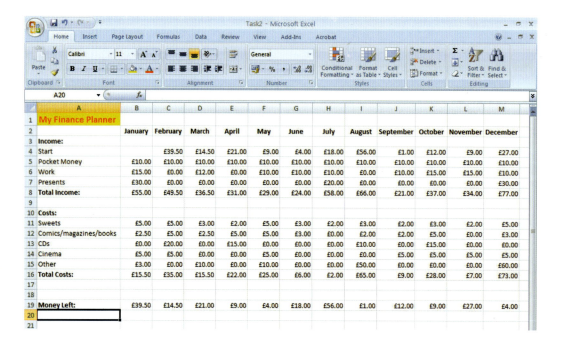

Figure 2.17

STEP 4: ANALYSING THE DATA

Now that you have set up a budget for the year, it would be good to analyse it to find out things such as:

❯ The number of months you plan to buy CDs

❯ The number of months you plan to go to the cinema

❯ The average amount you are going to spend each month as well as the maximum and minimum amounts.

These can easily be found using Excel's built-in functions but it would be a good idea to put these results on another worksheet.

Using the AVERAGE function

 1 Either double click on the Sheet1 tab at the bottom of the window or right click on it and select **Rename** from the menu.

Figure 2.18

2 Rename it as 'Data'.

3 Rename Sheet2 as 'Analysis' and then open it by selecting the tab.

We are going to show all of the data such as the number of CDs and the average costs per month on this sheet.

4 In cell A1 put the title for this sheet as 'Analysis of spending'.

You can format it how you wish and then change the width of column A so that the title does not overflow into column B. (You did this in Task 1, page 15).

5 In cell A3 put the label 'Average cost per month' and then make cell C3 the active cell.

In cell C3 we are going to place a function to find the average of the Total Costs row which is row 16.

43

6 Click the **Formulas** tab and then the arrow to the right of Autosum as shown in Figure 2.19.

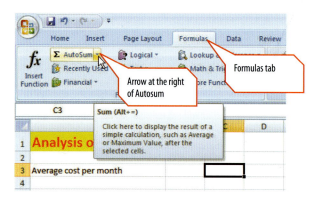

Figure 2.19

 7 Select **Average** from the menu.

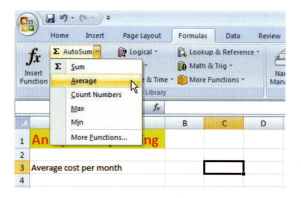

Figure 2.20

The Average function will now be inserted into cell C3 as shown in Figure 2.21.

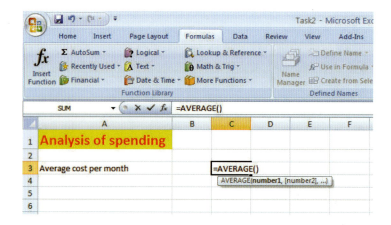

Figure 2.21

But what is it working out the average of? We now need to tell the function what it has to find the average of. Let's tell it that it needs to find the average of the total costs, i.e what we spend on average each month.

 8 Click on the **Data** tab to move back to the Data sheet and then highlight the Total Costs row from column B to column M as shown in Figure 2.22.

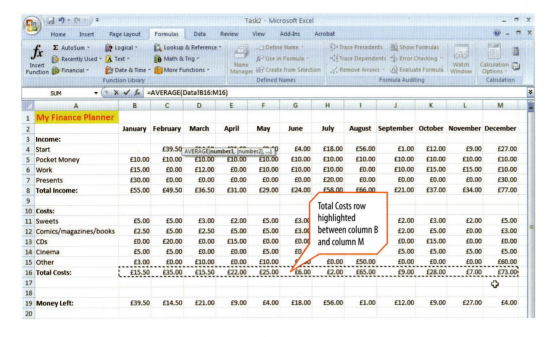

Figure 2.22

 9 Now press **Enter** or click the tick icon to the left of the formula bar.

You will be returned to the Analysis sheet and the average will be in cell C3 as shown in Figure 2.23.

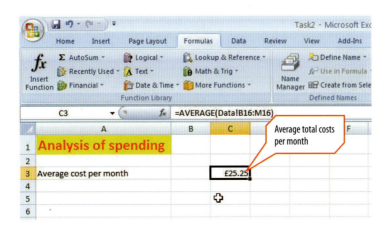

Figure 2.23

According to this spreadsheet model, you spend an average of £25.25 each month!

Now let's work out the maximum and the minimum amounts you have spent in a month.

Using the MAX and MIN functions

10 Follow instructions 6–9 to insert the Maximum and Minimum of the Total Costs row in cells C4 and C5 using the **Max** and **Min** functions. The Analysis sheet should now be similar to that shown in Figure 2.24.

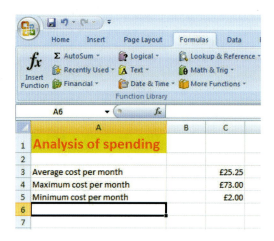

Figure 2.24

This shows you that you have spent as much as £73.00 (all those Christmas presents!) and as little as £2 in any one month (you must have been on holiday!).

Check on the Data sheet that these actually are the correct maximum and minimum amounts.

11 Now find the average, maximum and minimum for the monthly income so that the Analysis sheet looks like that shown in Figure 2.25.

IMPORTANT TIP
Don't forget to use the range in row 8 between columns B and M.

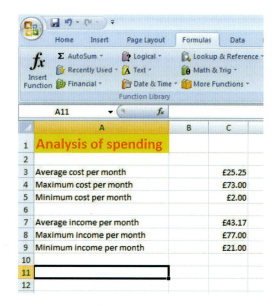

Figure 2.25

Great – now that you have learnt how to ask a few questions like 'in which cell is the highest (maximum) or lowest (minimum) amount?' about the data on your spreadsheet, let's find out how to ask some more!

We are now going to ask questions like 'how many cells contain this type of data?' so we are going to analyse the number of months in which you plan to buy CDs or go to the cinema.

This time we're going to use the COUNTIF function. To find out the number of months in which you plan to buy CDs we need to get Excel to look along row 13 and count how many cells have a value greater than zero.

Using the COUNTIF function

 12 Make cell A11 of the Analysis sheet the active cell and enter the label 'Number of months when CDs are bought'.

 13 We must now enter the function to carry out the count in cell C11.

> Make cell C11 the active cell.

> Select the **Formulas** tab.

> Click on **More Functions** > **Statistical**.

> Select **COUNTIF**.

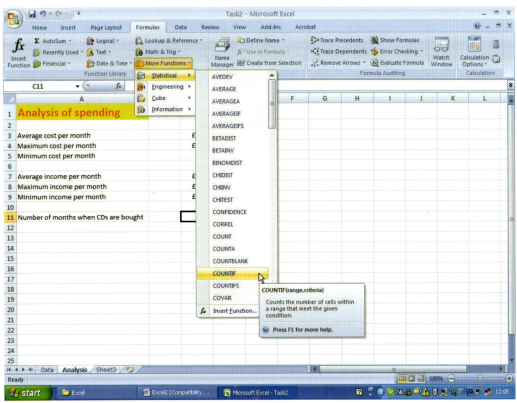

Figure 2.26

You will be shown the following dialogue box where you can tell Excel what you want to count.

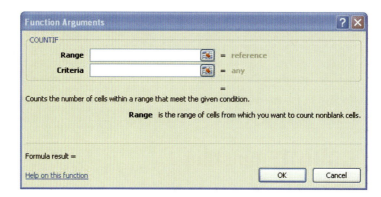

Figure 2.27

This dialogue box allows us to enter two things: the **range** and the **criteria**.

The range is the cells that Excel has to look at and the criteria is what Excel is looking for in those cells.

 Click on the icon at the right of the **Range** box as shown in Figure 2.28.

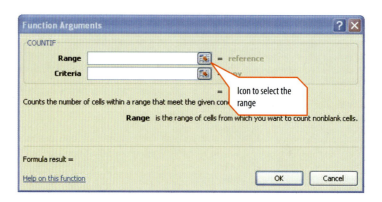

Figure 2.28

15 Now change to the Data sheet using the tabs at the bottom of the worksheet and drag along row 13 from column B to column M as shown in Figure 2.29.

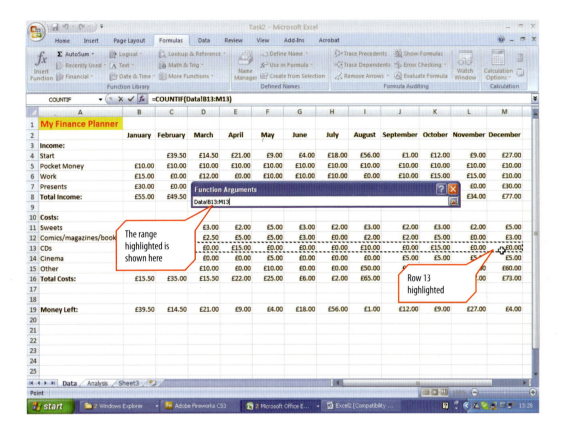

Figure 2.29

Click again on the icon at the right of the box to accept this range.

 16 Now we need to enter what you want Excel to look for in the **Criteria** box. We want to count the number of cells which have a value greater than zero – this means that you have bought CDs in this month.

Therefore insert **>0** in the **Criteria** box. This means **greater than** 0. It means that you have spent some money on a CD.

Figure 2.30

17 Click on **OK** and you should see the result of the function in cell C11 of the Analysis sheet.

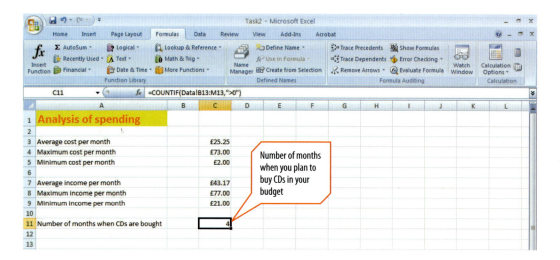

Figure 2.31

 18 Change to the Data sheet and check that the number is correct.

 19 Now follow instructions 13–17 to place the number of months with cinema visits into cell C12 as shown in Figure 2.32.

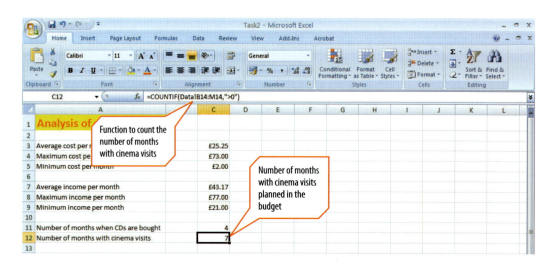

Figure 2.32

So this tells you that you plan to buy CDs in four months and go to the cinema in seven months of the year.

STEP 5: LOOKING FOR PATTERNS IN THE DATA

We can also analyse the spreadsheet by using **conditional formatting**. This allows us to fill cells with colour when they contain particular values.

In this example we could colour the cinema and CD cells when their value is greater than zero so that we could see if there were any times of the year when we bought more CDs or visited the cinema more.

Using conditional formatting

 Highlight row 13 of the Data sheet from column B to column M as shown in Figure 2.33.

	January	February	March	April	May	June	July	August	September	October	November	December
1 My Finance Planner												
3 Income:												
4 Start		£39.50	£14.50	£21.00	£9.00	£4.00	£18.00	£56.00	£1.00	£12.00	£9.00	£27.00
5 Pocket Money	£10.00	£10.00	£10.00	£10.00	£10.00	£10.00	£10.00	£10.00	£10.00	£10.00	£10.00	£10.00
6 Work	£15.00	£0.00	£12.00	£0.00	£10.00	£10.00	£10.00	£0.00	£10.00	£15.00	£15.00	£10.00
7 Presents	£30.00	£0.00	£0.00	£0.00	£0.00	£0.00	£20.00	£0.00	£0.00	£0.00	£0.00	£30.00
8 Total Income:	£55.00	£49.50	£36.50	£31.00	£29.00	£24.00	£58.00	£66.00	£21.00			£77.00
10 Costs:												
11 Sweets	£5.00	£5.00	£3.00	£2.00	£5.00	£3.00	£2.00	£3.00				£5.00
12 Comics/magazines/books	£2.50	£5.00	£2.50	£5.00	£5.00	£3.00	£0.00	£2.00		£5.00	£0.00	£3.00
13 CDs	£0.00	£20.00	£0.00	£15.00	£0.00	£0.00	£0.00	£10.00	£0.00	£15.00	£0.00	£0.00
14 Cinema	£5.00	£5.00	£0.00	£0.00	£5.00	£0.00	£0.00	£0.00	£0.00	£5.00	£5.00	£5.00
15 Other	£3.00	£0.00	£10.00	£0.00	£10.00	£0.00	£0.00	£50.00	£0.00	£0.00	£0.00	£60.00
16 Total Costs:	£15.50	£35.00	£15.50	£22.00	£25.00	£6.00	£2.00	£65.00	£9.00	£28.00	£7.00	£73.00
19 Money Left:	£39.50	£14.50	£21.00	£9.00	£4.00	£18.00	£56.00	£1.00	£12.00	£9.00	£27.00	£4.00

Row 13 highlighted

Figure 2.33

 From the **Home** tab select **Conditional Formatting** > **New Rule** as shown in Figure 2.34.

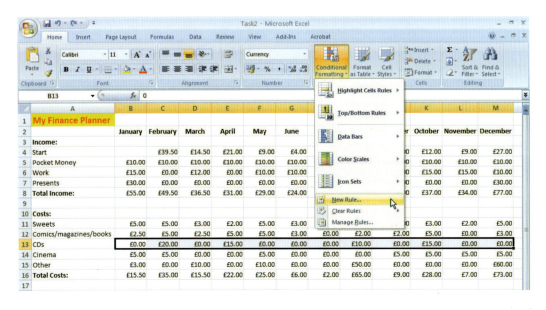

Figure 2.34

You will be shown the **New Formatting Rule** dialogue box. We need to use this dialogue box to format cells that contain values greater than zero.

3 Select **Format only cells that contain** from the list at the top of the dialogue box as shown in Figure 2.35.

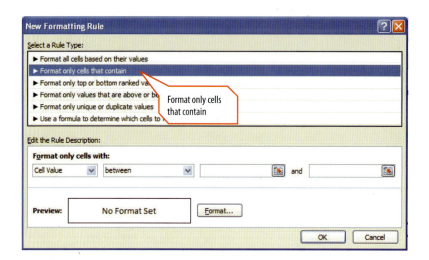

Figure 2.35

We now need to set the rule so that only cells in the range that contain a value greater than zero are formatted.

4 Select **greater than** from the rule drop-down box as shown in Figure 2.36.

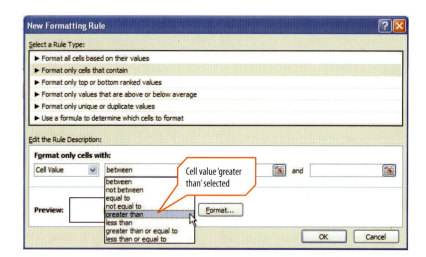

Figure 2.36

Now we need to tell Excel what the value should be.

5 Enter **0** as shown in Figure 2.37.

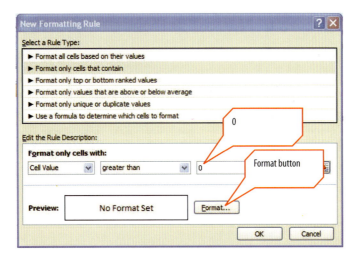

Figure 2.37

We must now tell Excel how to format the cell.

6 Click on the **Format** button to display the **Format Cells** dialogue box.

Select the **Fill** tab and select the red colour as shown in Figure 2.38.

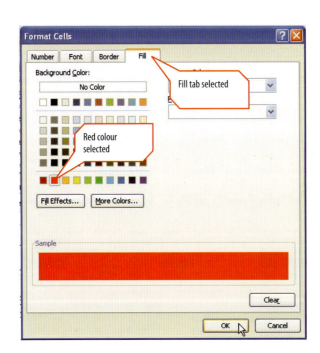

Figure 2.38

7 Click on **OK** and then the OK button of the **New Formatting Rule** dialogue box and the cells in row 13 which have a value greater than zero should be filled with red as shown in Figure 2.39.

Months where money is to be spent on CDs have a red background

Figure 2.39

You can now look for any patterns in the data. For example, in Figure 2.39 you can see that on two occasions, CDs are going to be bought in the month after a present has been received.

We can now use conditional formatting for planned cinema visits.

8 Highlight row 14 between columns B and M and then follow instructions 2–7 above, but this time select blue for the fill colour. Your spreadsheet should now look like that shown in Figure 2.40.

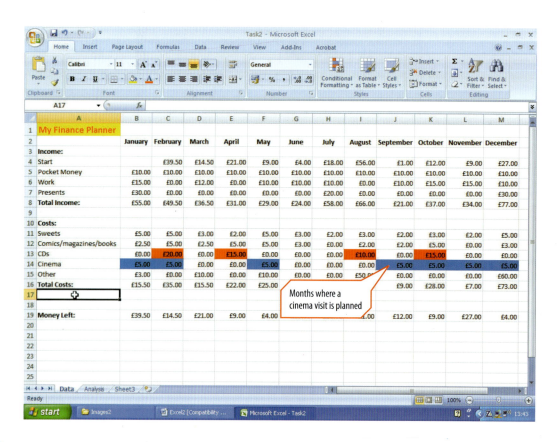

Months where a cinema visit is planned

Figure 2.40

It looks as though more cinema visits are planned for winter months and none in the summer months of June, July and August. Maybe there are no planned film releases for these months or there are better things to do during these months when it is warm.

You can apply conditional formatting to look for other patterns, for example months where presents are expected or where the total income is expected to be over £50.

CHECKPOINT

You should be able to:

> Protect selected cells in a spreadsheet.

> Unprotect a spreadsheet.

> Insert rows into a spreadsheet.

> Delete data in a spreadsheet.

> Use the SUM function.

> Use the AVERAGE function.

> Use the MAX function.

> Use the MIN function.

> Use the COUNTIF function.

> Use conditional formatting.

ASSESSMENT POINT

Now let's assess the work. Look back at the table at the beginning of this section (**Target Point**) and decide on which of the statements you can answer 'Yes' to.

Did you do as well as you expected? Could you improve your work? Add a comment to your work to show what you could do to improve it so that next time you'll remember to do it the first time.

TASK BRIEF

Your spreadsheet needs to be able to show you how income and costs vary from month to month, using graphs and charts.

Your spreadsheet now allows you to show more details about income and costs and to carry out some analysis – it is starting to look like a professional financial model. However, it is sometimes difficult to see how the income and costs vary from month to month just by looking at a table of figures and so most financial reports display the results in the form of graphs and charts.

Your task is to display your budget by:

 creating a column chart to show the costs month by month

 creating a line graph to display the total income and the total costs over the year.

As you create the spreadsheet model, you will cover the following:

SOFTWARE SKILLS

You will learn how to:

> Select cell ranges to be included in the chart or graph

> Create column charts

> Create line graphs

> Format charts and graphs

FUNCTIONAL SKILLS

As you work through this task the Functional Skills tabs will explain to you why the task tackles the brief in the way shown here and explain why you would choose to:

> Create charts and graphs

CAPABILITY

You will show that you can:

> Select a data series to produce a column chart or line graph

> Create column charts and line graphs

> Format the charts and graphs and add titles that make them meaningful for an audience

VOCABULARY

You should learn these new words and understand what they mean.

> Column chart

> Line graph

> Axes

RESOURCES

There is one file for this task that demonstrates what you will be creating in Excel:

Task3.xlsx

If you want to take a look at this file before you start you can download it from www.payne-gallway.co.uk

Level 3	Level 4	Level 5
You have saved the file with a new name. You saved it as 'Task3'	You have saved the file with a new name in a new folder	You have created a line graph to show the relationship between the total income and the total costs
You have saved the file in the correct folder	You have selected a data set and created an appropriate graph or chart	
You have created a column chart		

TARGET POINT

Have a look at the following statements before you start your task so you know what you are aiming for.

Although you will not be making your own decisions for much of this activity, these levels show you what you could be awarded when completing similar tasks on other work where you are working more independently and without following instructions.

OK. Let's get started.

Before you start any task, you should organise your area where you are going to save the work.

 Create a new folder inside the 'Excel' folder and name it Task3 – this is where you will save the file you will be creating in this task.

 Open the Task2 worksheet and use 'Save As' to rename the file as **Task3** and save it in the Task3 folder.

STEP 1: CREATING A COLUMN CHART TO SHOW THE COSTS EACH MONTH

We will use a new worksheet for the chart and graph so that the others do not become too crowded.

 Rename Sheet3 as 'Charts'. (You renamed a sheet in Task 2 on page 43).

Selecting cell ranges

 Make the Data sheet the active sheet and highlight the row that contains the month labels from column A to column M as shown in Figure 3.1.

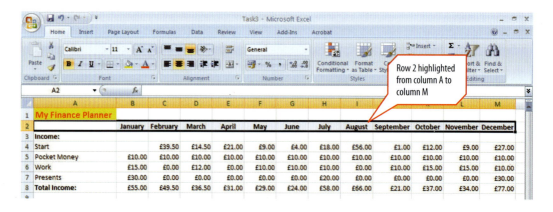

Figure 3.1

 Hold down the **Ctrl** key and also highlight the costs rows from cell A11 to cell M15, as shown in Figure 3.2.

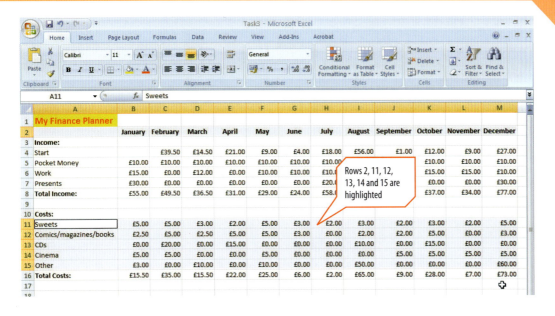

Figure 3.2

TIP

Holding down the control key while you highlight cells, means you can highlight cells that are not side-by-side

Creating a column chart

 Select the **Insert** tab, click the arrow under the **Column** type and select the first **2-D Column** chart, as shown in Figure 3.3.

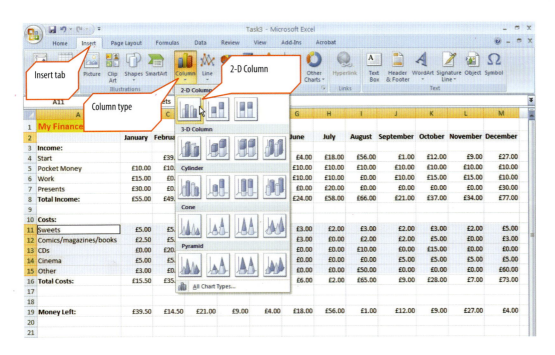

Figure 3.3

The column chart will now be drawn on the sheet as shown in Figure 3.4.

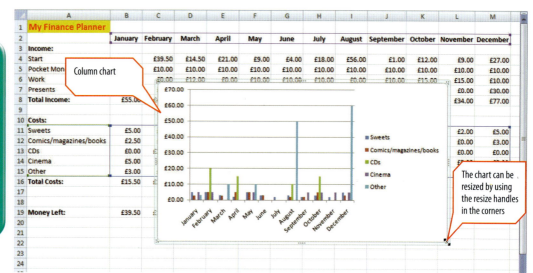

Figure 3.4

When the chart is selected, three new tabs appear on the ribbon as shown in Figure 3.5.

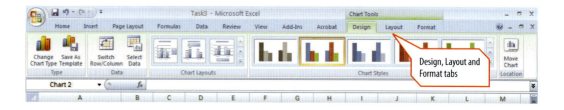

Figure 3.5

The **Design** tab is currently selected.

5 Click on the arrow at the bottom of the **Chart Styles** group and you will see some different chart styles for you to select.

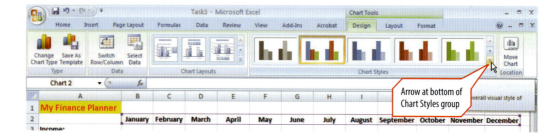

Figure 3.6

You will now see the different styles that you can select as shown in Figure 3.7.

Figure 3.7

Select a style of your choice and the chart will appear in that style.

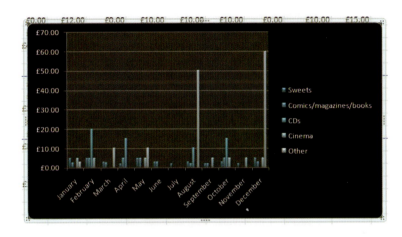

Figure 3.8

We've converted our table of data into a chart, but to make it more meaningful the chart needs a title. This can be added by selecting the **Layout** tab.

 Select the **Layout** tab and click on the arrow below **Chart Title** in the **Labels** group and select **Above Chart** as shown in Figure 3.9.

FUNCTIONAL SKILLS

Labelling charts and graphs – just as for your spreadsheet data, labelling your charts and graphs is important because labels tell you what the graph is showing. Each graph or chart should have a main title, a title for each axis and a legend

Figure 3.9

The title frame will appear above the chart.

 7 Click in the title frame, delete the text and type in 'Costs per month' as the title as shown in Figure 3.10.

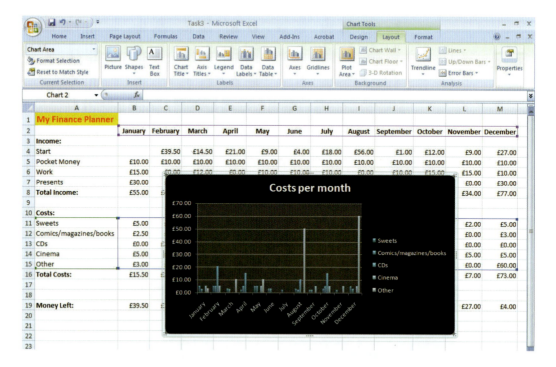

Figure 3.10

SOFTWARE SKILLS
Adding axis titles

8 Click on the arrow below the **Axis Titles** icon in the **Labels** group to add titles to the horizontal and vertical axes as shown in Figure 3.11.

Figure 3.11

9 Now select **Primary Horizontal Axis Title** and select **Title Below Axis** as shown in Figure 3.12.

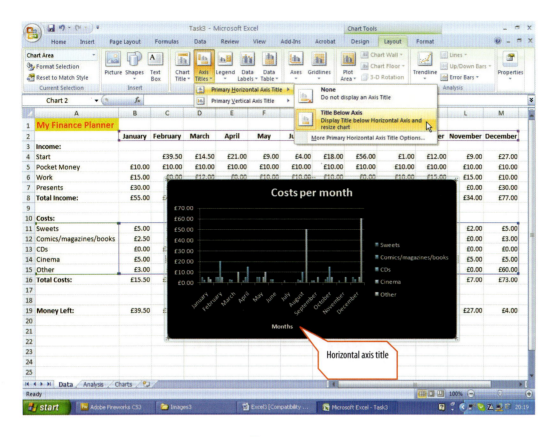

Figure 3.12

Insert 'Months' as the label.

Now that we have labelled our chart correctly and it makes sense to our audience, we can now move the chart to the Charts sheet so that it isn't sitting on top of our data table.

 10 Right click on the chart and select **Move Chart** from the menu.

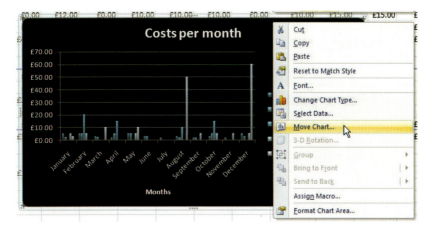

Figure 3.13

11 Select the **Charts** sheet from the drop-down list as shown in Figure 3.14 and click on **OK**.

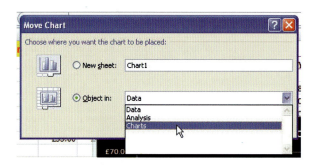

Figure 3.14

Turn to the Charts sheet and position the chart. That's our first chart completed – now let's see how we create a line graph.

STEP 2: CREATING A LINE GRAPH TO COMPARE TOTAL INCOME AND COSTS OVER THE YEAR

1 Make the Data sheet the active sheet and highlight row 2 from column A to column M as you did for the previous chart. This will select the months.

2 Hold down the **Ctrl** key and highlight rows 8 and 16 to select the total income and the total costs for each month.

3 Now select the **Insert** tab and **Line** > **2D Line** as shown in Figure 3.15.

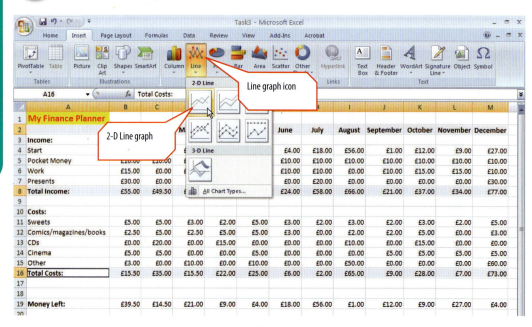

Figure 3.15

4 Use the **Layout** tab to insert chart and axis titles as shown in Figure 3.16.

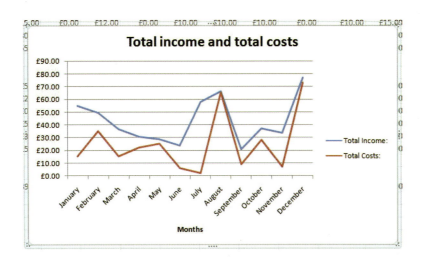

Figure 3.16

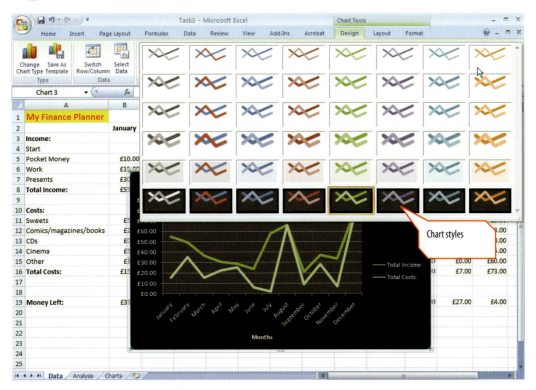 **5** Use the **Design** tab to select chart style as you did in Step 1.

Figure 3.17

Move the graph to the Chart sheet as you did in Step 1. You should now be able to see your graph and chart side by side.

By converting your data into charts, it's now much easier to see trends in your income and spending. Looks like lots of presents were bought in December!

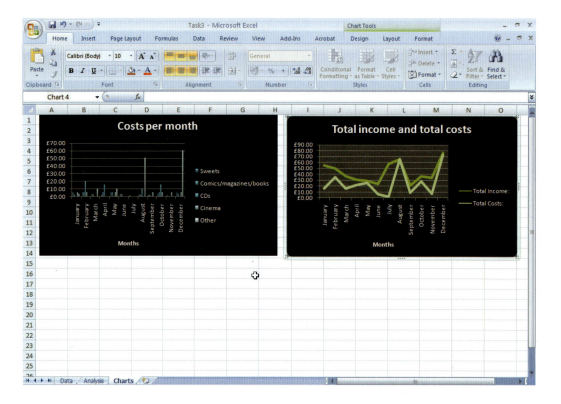

Figure 3.18

CHECKPOINT

You should be able to:

> Select data ranges for charts and graphs.

> Create a column chart.

> Add a chart title.

> Add an axis title.

> Move a chart to another sheet.

> Create a line graph.

ASSESSMENT POINT

Now let's assess the work. Look back at the table at the beginning of this section (**Target Point**) and decide on which of the statements you can answer 'Yes' to.

Did you do as well as you expected? Could you improve your work? Add a comment to your work to show what you could do to improve it so that next time you'll remember to do it the first time.

TASK BRIEF

You need to adjust your spreadsheet model to allow you to budget for monthly savings, to work out which bikes you will be able to afford.

So far your spreadsheet model:

❯ shows details of your income and costs

❯ contains conditional formatting to highlight data in particular cells

❯ includes charts which make it much easier to see trends in your income and spending.

But now we want it to show your plans for saving money each month.

Your parents have agreed that you can have a new bike for your next Christmas present – but only if you save enough money to pay a quarter of the cost!

So your task is to budget for monthly savings by including in the model:

 the costs of bikes you would like and how much you would have to contribute for each

 the percentage of your monthly income you could save.

You will then be able to use the model to experiment with different percentage savings to see which bike you will be able to afford by saving either less or more, but remember you cannot go into the red in any month!

As you create the spreadsheet model, you will cover the following:

SOFTWARE SKILLS

You will learn how to:

▶ Insert a new worksheet

▶ Format cells to show percentages

▶ Use absolute cell references

▶ Use the VLOOKUP function

▶ Format a number for the number of decimal places

▶ Use the IF function

▶ Format the border around a group of cells

FUNCTIONAL SKILLS

As you work through this task the Functional Skills tabs will explain to you why the task tackles the brief in the way shown here and explain why you would choose to:

▶ Change the number of decimal places

▶ Use absolute and relative cell references

▶ Use a border around a group of cells

CAPABILITY

You will show that you can:

▶ Develop a model that will transfer data from one worksheet to another

▶ Develop a model that uses absolute cell references

▶ Develop a model that can predict how much should be saved to meet a specified target

VOCABULARY

You should learn these new words and understand what they mean.

▶ Percentage

▶ VLookup

▶ Integer

▶ Absolute formula

TARGET POINT

Have a look at the following statements before you start your task so you know what you are aiming for.

Although you will not be making your own decisions for much of this activity, these levels show you what you could be awarded when completing similar tasks on other work where you are working more independently and without following instructions.

Level 3	Level 4	Level 5	Level 6
You have saved the file with a new name. You saved it as 'Task4'	You have saved the file with a new name in a new folder	You have used an absolute cell reference	You have used the VLOOKUP function
	You have added a new worksheet to the workbook, labelled it correctly and added data to it about the bikes		You have used the IF function
	You have formatted a cell to show percentages		You have used the model to predict your monthly savings to be able to afford one of the bikes
	You have changed the number of decimal places		

OK. Let's get started.

Before you start any task, you should organise your area where you are going to save the work.

 Create a new folder inside the 'Excel' folder and call it Task4 – this is where you will save the file you will be creating in this task.

 Open the Task2 worksheet and use 'Save As' to rename the File as **Task4** and save it in the Task4 folder.

STEP 1: INSERTING DATA ABOUT A BIKE INTO THE DATA SHEET

You have done some research and have found suitable bikes that you would like for your Christmas present. You have found bikes of different prices ranging from £85 to £300 so you will be able to use the budget model to see which you will be able to afford. Remember, you have to pay a quarter of the cost!

You have found the six suitable bikes:

Name of bike	Price
Speed Anger Mountain	£300
Mustang	£200
Crusader Dirt Trax	£180
Mountain Dynamic	£120
Mud Cruncher	£100
Basic Mountain	£85

We must create a new worksheet to store this data.

Inserting a worksheet

 Click on the **Insert Worksheet** tab to the right of the Charts tab to create a new worksheet.

Figure 4.1

2 Rename the new worksheet as 'Bikes' (you renamed sheets in Task 2 on page 43) and make it the active sheet.

On the **Bikes** worksheet enter the data as shown in Figure 4.2.

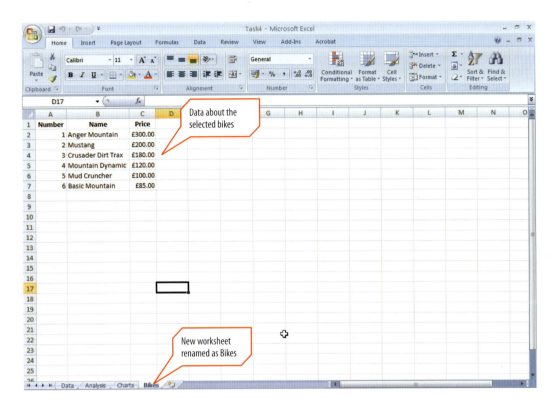

Figure 4.2

IMPORTANT TIP:
On the worksheet there is an extra column so that each bike has a number.

Now we are going to transfer data about the specific bikes we select to the main data sheet from the bike sheet without typing it in. We are going to use a function called **VLOOKUP** to do this.

Using the VLOOKUP function

Let's start.

  Make the **Data** sheet the active sheet and insert 'Bike' as the label in cell A21 as shown in Figure 4.3.

Figure 4.3

When we have finished we will be able to enter any of the bike numbers (1–6) into cell B21 and Excel will automatically put the correct name of the bike in cell C21 and the price in cell E21 for us. Great!

So we're going to need to tell Excel where to find the instructions from us about which bike we want information on (cell B21) and insert functions in cells C21 and E21 to transfer data about that bike from the Bike sheet to the Data sheet. OK so far?

  Make cell C21 the active cell and select the **Formulas** tab > **Lookup & Reference** > **VLOOKUP** as shown in Figure 4.4.

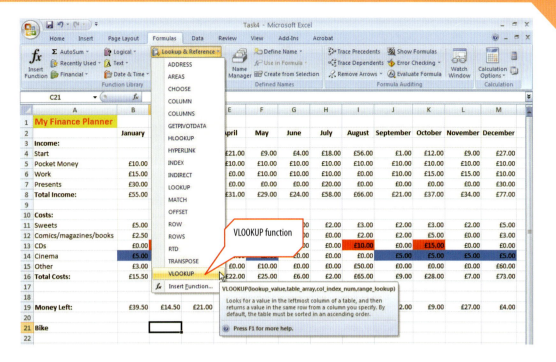

Figure 4.4

You will see the **Function Arguments** dialogue box displayed. This box wants us to include:

> the cell reference of where it can find the instructions from us

> the cell references of the table where Excel has to 'look up' the information from

> the column number within the table that gives the exact information we want.

Don't worry, we're going to go through this. Let's look at how we do it.

Click on the icon at the right of the **Lookup_value** input box as shown in Figure 4.5.

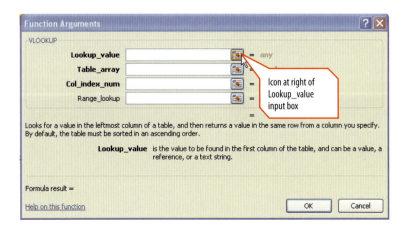

Figure 4.5

Click on cell B21 and then click on the icon at the right of the input box as shown in Figure 4.6.

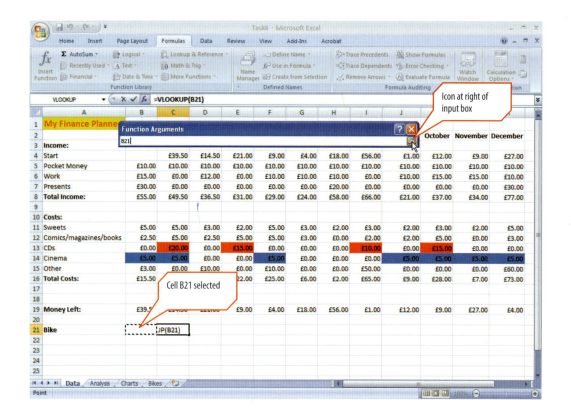

Figure 4.6

Excel now knows where to find the instructions from us about which bike to look up.

You will be returned to the **Function Arguments** dialogue box.

We must now tell Excel where the table is that it has to 'look up' the information from.

 To show Excel where the table is:

> Click on the icon at the right of the **Table_array** input box.

> Click on the Bikes tab at the bottom of the worksheet to make this the active sheet.

> Highlight the whole of the table as shown in Figure 4.7 and you will see top-left and bottom-right cell references in the input box.

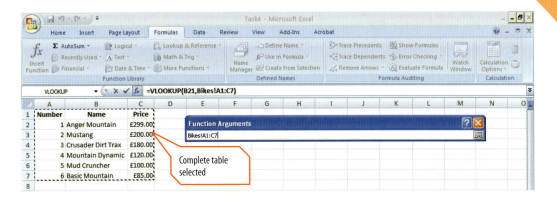

Figure 4.7

➤ Click on the icon at the right of the input box to return to the **Function Arguments** dialogue box.

Excel now knows where to find the table of information.

We must now tell Excel which column of the table it must get the data from. As we want to insert the name of the bike in cell C21, we must tell it to get the data from the second column, column 2, because that's the column with the bike names in.

 Enter **2** in the **Col_index_num** input box as shown in Figure 4.8.

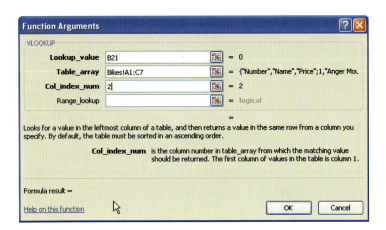

Figure 4.8

9 Now click in the **OK** box to set the function and you will see the result of the function in cell C21.

It's not the name of a bike though! You should see an error message instead, as shown in Figure 4.9.

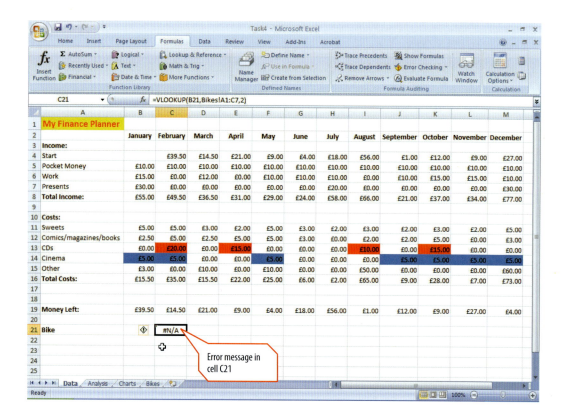

Figure 4.9

We are getting an error message because there is no number in cell B21.

We told Excel to:

▶ get the number from cell B21 and then

▶ look down the first column of the data table in the Bikes sheet until it found that number and then

▶ get the data from the second column of that row and then

▶ put it in cell C21.

It cannot do that because there is no number in cell B21.

10 So enter the number **3** into cell B21.

Crusader Dirt Trax should now appear in cell C21.

Figure 4.10

Yes, it works! Well done.

But we have another problem. Cell B21 is formatted for currency and it shows £3.00 instead of just the number 3.

11 Make cell B21 the active cell, select the **Home** tab, click the arrow to the right of the **Format** box in the **Number** group as shown in Figure 4.11 and select **Number**.

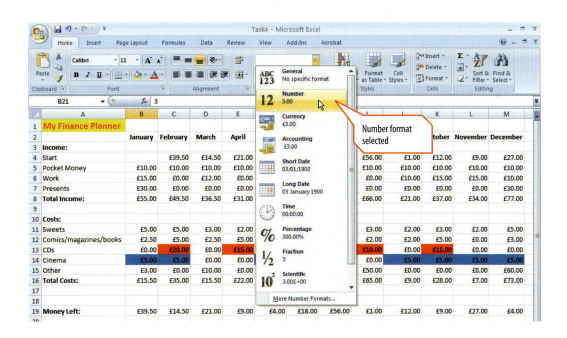

Figure 4.11

The number in cell B21 now appears as 3.00. We want it to show as an integer (whole number) and we don't want any decimal places.

FUNCTIONAL SKILLS

Changing the number of decimal places – the number of decimal places you use depends on how accurate you need your information to be, e.g. do you need to know that the answer is £2.34, or would £2.30 or even £2 be good enough?

Formatting a number for the number of decimal places

 We can easily make it into an integer by clicking on the **Decrease Decimal** icon in the **Number** group of tools as shown in Figure 4.12.

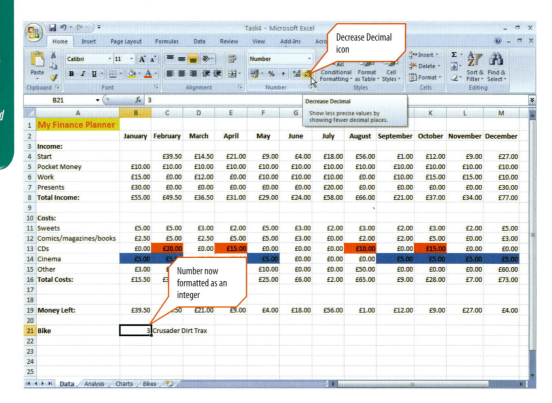

Figure 4.12

Great – we're nearly there, but remember, we wanted to add the price in cell E21 too.

Now it's over to you …

 Make cell E21 the active cell and follow instructions 4–8 above to get Excel to take the price of the bike from the table on the Bikes sheet and insert it into cell E21 on the main data sheet.

> **IMPORTANT TIP**
>
> *Remember to put the number 3 into the Col_index_num input box as we want the information from the third column.*

When you have inserted the VLOOKUP function you should see the following in cell E21.

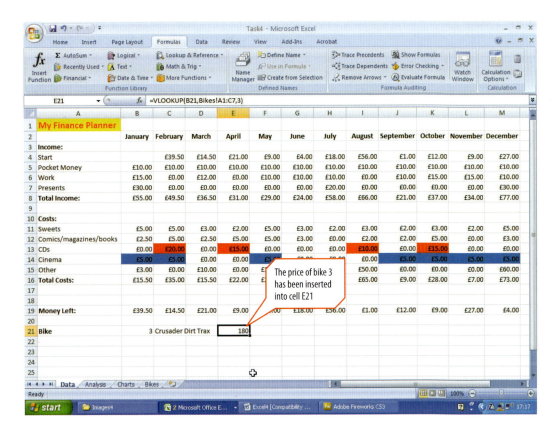

Figure 4.13

Yes, it works. Well done!

All we have to do to finish this section is to format this cell for currency.

If you have forgotten how to do this, look back at Task 1, page 25.

 One last thing before you've completed this part of the model, test the VLOOKUP functions by placing different numbers into cell B21.

The contents of cells C21 and E21 should change as you do this.

If you enter a number greater than 6, details of bike number 6 are displayed.

All done!

STEP 2: CALCULATING HOW MUCH WE HAVE TO SAVE

Now to the big question – how much are we going to need to save? Remember we have to save enough to pay a quarter of the cost of whichever bike we choose.

So we're going to calculate the savings needed for each bike.

 Enter the label '**Savings Target**' into cell A22.

We must now enter a formula into cell B22 to calculate how much we need to save for the price of the bike shown in cell E21. This is the price of the bike divided by four.

 Make cell B22 the active cell and enter the following formula:

$$=E21/4$$

Check that the formula works. If you select bike number 1, then the Savings target should be £75 – that is £300 divided by 4.

STEP 3: CALCULATING THE PERCENTAGE OF OUR INCOME WE SHOULD SAVE

Now we know what our savings target is for each bike, the next step is to calculate what our savings could be. This will be a percentage of our monthly income.

We are going to get the spreadsheet to allow us to enter the percentage of our total monthly income we would like to save in cell H21, then calculate what the total savings would be over the year and show them as part of our costs. Let's make a start.

SOFTWARE SKILLS

Formatting a cell for percentage

Formatting a cell for percentage

 Enter the label '**% Savings**' in cell G21 of the Data sheet.

 We are now going to enter possible values in cell H21. Remember it's percentages that we're entering so you should only enter numbers between 1 and 100.

Before we enter any values, though, we need to format cell H21 so that Excel will know that the values we are entering have to be treated as percentages.

 Make cell H21 the active cell.

 Select the **Home** tab and click the arrow at the right of the **Format** box in the **Number** group as shown in Figure 4.14, then select **Number**.

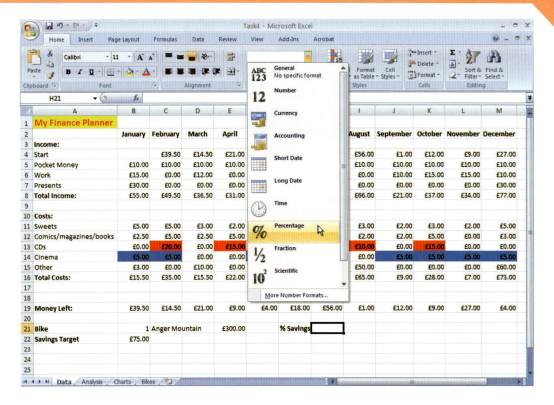

Figure 4.14

Try it out. Enter the number **10** into cell H21. It should be shown with a percentage sign as shown in Figure 4.15.

Figure 4.15

Excel is going to use the value we enter in H21 to calculate the savings amount each month. This amount will be added into the total costs so we need to make space for it.

 Make cell A16 the active cell and insert a row. You should remember how to do this as we inserted rows in Task 2 (pages 36–37).

Enter '**Savings**' as the new label in cell A16 as shown in Figure 4.16.

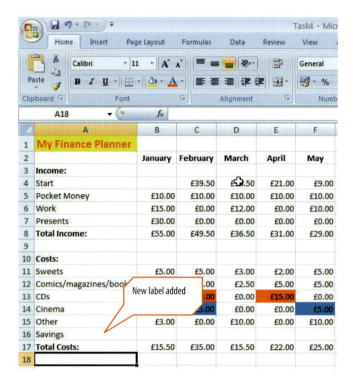

Figure 4.16

Now we need to work out how to calculate the savings amount so we need a new rule for the spreadsheet. The rule we will use is: Total Income × percentage savings value, e.g. £55 × 10%.

 Make cell B16 the active cell and enter the following formula.

=B8*H21

This will multiply the total income for January by the percentage savings value to calculate the savings for that month.

 Check that the formula is correct. The value shown in cell B16 should be 10% of the value shown in cell B8 – that is the value in B8 divided by 10. The total income shown in B8 is £55 and the savings shown is £5.50, so it's correct – great.

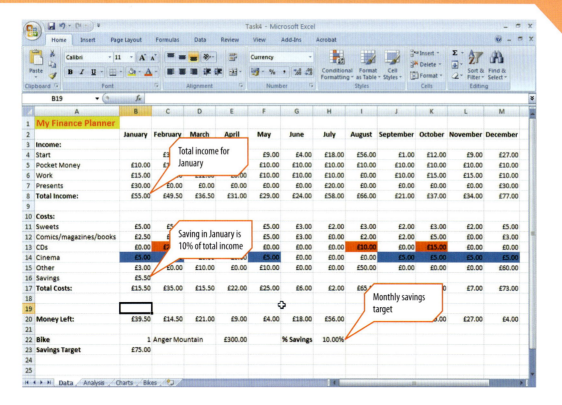

Figure 4.17

 Let's make life easy and use the fill handle to fill the formula in cell A16, all the way along row 16 up to column M as shown in Figure 4.18.

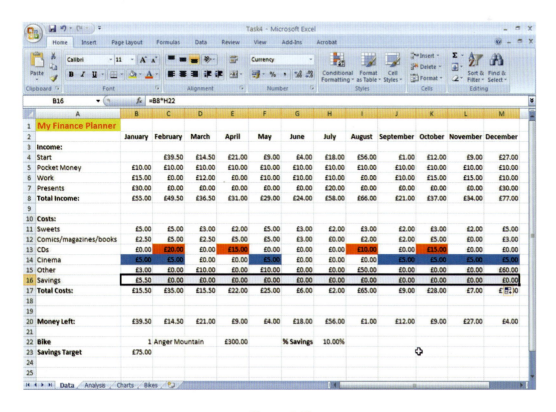

Figure 4.18

That doesn't seem right! It is showing the savings as £0.00 for all the months from February to December. For February it should be £4.95 and for December it should be £7.70.

There seems to be an error in our spreadsheet. We will have to debug it!

The first thing we should do is check the formulas in the cells along row 16.

 Make cell C16 the active cell and look at the formula. Then do the same for all the cells along row 16. They should be like the ones shown in the following table:

Cell	Formula
B16	=B8*H22
C16	=C8*I22
D16	=D8*J22
E16	=E8*K22
F16	=F8*L22
G16	=G8*M22
H16	=H8*N22
I16	=I8*O22
J16	=J8*P22
K16	=K8*Q22
L16	=L8*R22
M16	=M8*S22

Can you see what the problem is?

Yes, that's correct. We should be multiplying the values shown in row 8 by the value shown in cell H22. H22 has changed to I22, J22, K22, etc., as we filled the formula along the row.

We don't want it to change though, we want it to stay the same because we are multiplying all of the monthly income values by the same cell. What we have to do is change it from a **relative** cell reference into an **absolute** cell reference.

Absolute cell references

IMPORTANT TIP

A cell reference that changes is called a relative cell reference.
A cell reference that does not change is called an absolute cell reference.

Let's look at what we have to do.

Here is the formula we entered into cell B16

$$=B8*H22$$

For our calculation we want B8 to change into C8, D8, etc., but we want H22 to stay the same for the entire row.

 11 Make cell B16 the active cell and enter the following formula:

$$=B8*\$H22$$

The **$** sign (Shift-4) tells Excel that it should not change the letter as the formula is filled along the row.

IMPORTANT TIP

You can also place a $ sign in front of the number if you are filling the formula vertically (down a column) and do not want the row number to change.

 12 Now use the fill handle of cell B16 to fill the formula along row 16.

Check that the savings values are now correct.

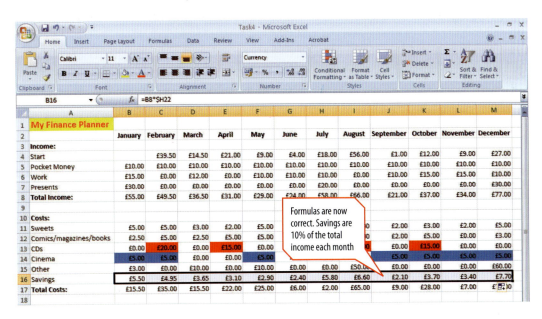

Figure 4.19

SOFTWARE SKILLS
Using absolute cell references

FUNCTIONAL SKILLS

Absolute cell references – if you use relative cell references when you copy a formula across several columns, the cell references change automatically to reflect the new columns. However, if you don't want the cell references to change because you want every column to use a particular cell in the calculation, then you would use an absolute cell reference to stop them automatically changing

STEP 4: ADDING THE SAVINGS INTO THE TOTAL COSTS

Our spreadsheet now looks correct, but look again. The Savings are not being included in the Total Costs – the Total Costs for January should be £21, not £15.50. Each time you add extra data to your spreadsheet you should check that your formulas are including all of the new data.

Checking and changing a function

 Make cell B17 the active cell and look at the formula in the formula bar as shown in Figure 4.20.

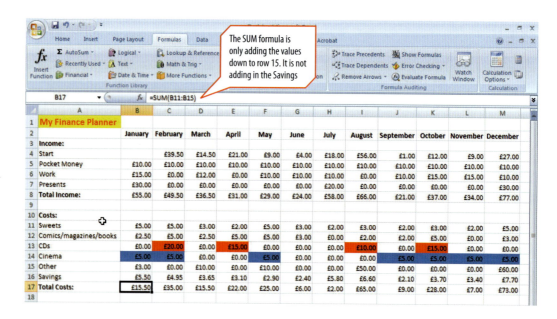

Figure 4.20

The formula reads:

=SUM(B11:B15)

But because we have added a row for savings, we need to change it so that the formula adds the values in cell **B16** too.

 Change the formula to:

=SUM(B11:B16)

 Now use the fill handle of cell B17 to fill the new formula along row 17 up to column M.

You will probably see lots of red on your spreadsheet, now that you have added in the savings. Don't worry about this for now – you can alter the figures later on.

Now we have worked out what our possible savings for each month could be, we now need the model to show us what our total savings will be if we save the percentage shown in cell H22 every month.

 16 Enter the label '**Total**' into cell G23.

 17 In cell H23 enter the SUM function to find the total of the cells along row 16 between columns B and M. You used the SUM function in Task 2 (page 39). The function should be:

=SUM(B16:M16)

The worksheet should now appear as that shown in Figure 4.21.

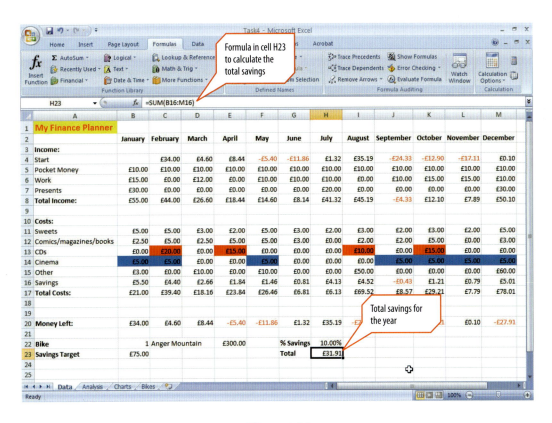

Figure 4.21

Now we have a model that will tell us how much we will save each month and the total we will save over the year according to the different percentages we enter into cell H22.

STEP 5: GETTING EXCEL TO CHECK IF WE HAVE SAVED ENOUGH FOR THE BIKE

Let's just recap over what our spreadsheet can do, because it's pretty clever! We can:

➤ choose different bikes and the spreadsheet will tell us the name and price of them

➤ work out a quarter of the price of each bike and therefore what we need to save

➤ choose different saving percentages

➤ work out our savings for each month and over the whole year.

That's quite a lot of information, but there's one last bit we need to work out. We need to make the spreadsheet compare our savings with the amount we need to save for each bike. We can't buy the bike if we haven't saved enough!

Let's see how we do that.

SOFTWARE SKILLS
Using the IF function

Using the IF function

We need to check that the value in cell H23 it is either the same as or higher than the value in cell B23 – this means that we have saved enough.

We could check this ourselves, but just to make absolutely sure we're right, let's get Excel to tell us.

So we're going to get the model to place a message in cell G24 which says either '**You have saved enough**' or '**You have not saved enough**'.

We do this using the **IF** function.

The rule for this function will be:

> **IF the value in cell H23 is greater than or equal to the value in cell B23 then return the message 'You have saved enough'.**

> **IF it is not then return the message 'You have not saved enough'.**

 Make cell G24 the active cell and select the **Formulas** tab > **Logical** > **IF** as shown in Figure 4.22.

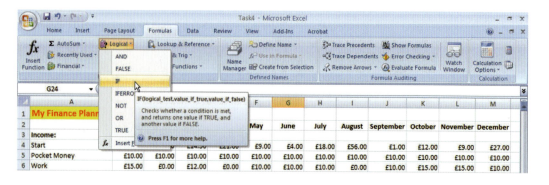

Figure 4.22

You will be shown the **Function Arguments** dialogue box as shown in Figure 4.23.

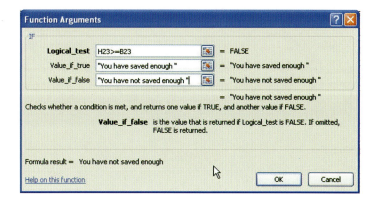

Figure 4.23

The first thing we need to do is to set the logical test. This is where we enter the formula that will compare the values in cells H23 and B23.

  Select the **Logical_test** input box and enter the following test:

H23>=B23

This means we are asking Excel to check IF the value in cell H23 is greater than or equal to the value in cell B23.

  Now select the **Value_if_true** input box and enter the following message:

"You have saved enough"

  Now select the **Value_if_false** input box and enter the following message:

"You have not saved enough"

The dialogue box should be like that shown in Figure 4.24.

Figure 4.24

5 Click on **OK** and you should see the result of the function in cell G24 as shown in Figure 4.25.

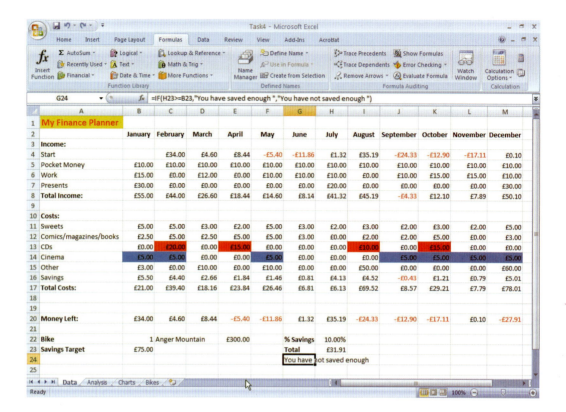

Figure 4.25

6 Experiment to see what happens if you select a cheaper bike by entering a different value in cell B22.

In the example shown in Figure 4.26, enough would be saved for bikes 4–6, although we've gone into the red because we haven't budgeted properly. You'll get to do that later on.

Figure 4.26

STEP 6: HIGHLIGHTING THE BIKE AREA OF THE SPREADSHEET

All of our calculations are done so all that's left is to improve the appearance of the spreadsheet by drawing a frame around the area at the bottom of the worksheet where the savings and bike details are displayed.

Formatting the border around a group of cells

 7 Highlight the cells from A21 to I25 as shown in Figure 4.27.

Figure 4.27

 8 Now select the **Home** tab > **Format** > **Format Cells** from the **Cells** group as shown in Figure 4.28.

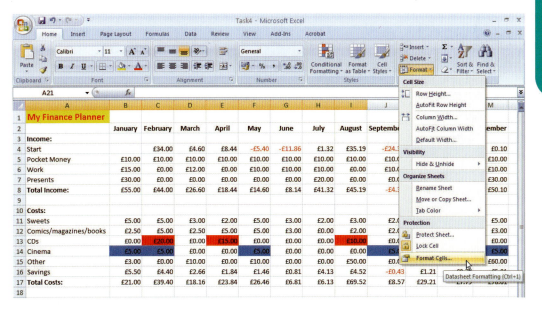

Figure 4.28

You will be shown the **Format Cells** dialogue box.

SOFTWARE SKILLS

Formatting the border around a group of cells

FUNCTIONAL SKILLS

Using borders – borders are used to make your spreadsheet easier to use because they can highlight certain areas or split columns and rows. You can make any of the gridlines into a border but that can make the spreadsheet look too complicated so choose carefully. Some of the borders you would normally see on a spreadsheet would be the outline of your table, the lines in between each column and a line under the headings

Select the **Border** tab and click on the **Outline** icon as shown in Figure 4.29.

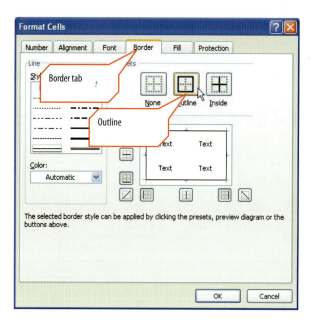

Figure 4.29

 You can select a different type or thickness of outline from the **Style** box and then click on the displayed outlines to change them as shown in Figure 4.30.

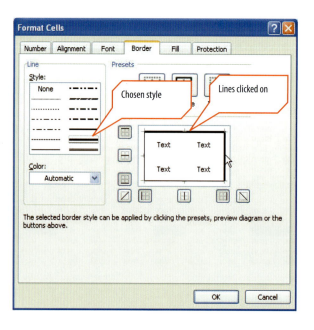

Figure 4.30

 Click on **OK**. The worksheet should now look like that shown in Figure 4.31.

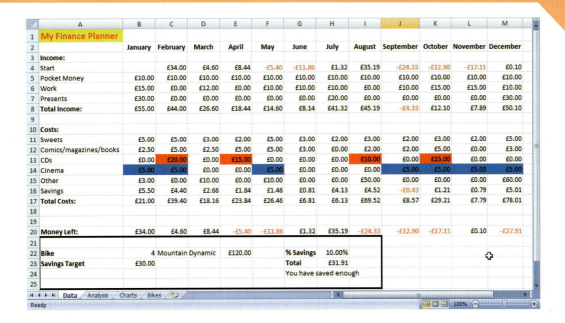

Figure 4.31

One last thing……You could protect the worksheet so that you do not accidentally enter numbers into any of the cells with formulas and functions.

You learned how to do this in Task 2 (pages 32–34).

 Remember you have to highlight the cells where you *will* want to change numbers and use the **Home** tab > **Format** > **Format Cells** in the **Cells** group and then the **Protection** tab to remove the tick from the **Locked** box.

The cells that should be unlocked are filled with yellow in Figure 4.32.

Figure 4.32

13 Finally select **Protect Sheet** from the **Home** tab > **Format** menu in the **Cells** group.

Excellent – you've completed your model. Now to the fun bit – putting in different values to try and work out which bike you can afford.

STEP 7: USING THE MODEL

You can now use the model to create your budget for the year.

Remember that you are not allowed to go into the red!

You will have to make some difficult decisions. Will you have a cheaper bike for Christmas and more CDs, magazines and trips to the cinema or will you have a better bike and spend less during the year?

You may decide to try to earn more money during the year or negotiate more pocket money.

Remember you can change the percentage of your total income you plan to save.

Try to be as realistic as possible.

Figure 4.33 shows that the user has decided to spend less on sweets, CDs and cinema visits and has changed the percentage savings to 11% so that they can choose Bike 2.

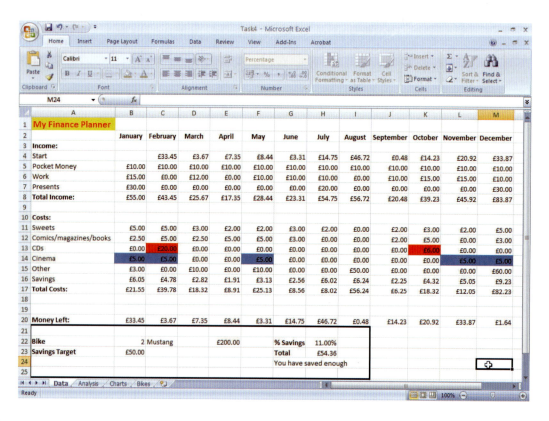

Figure 4.33

They could have decided to go for the cheapest bike and spend more on CDs and magazines during the year.

What will you choose?

CHECKPOINT

You should be able to:

> Insert and rename a new worksheet.

> Use the VLOOKUP function.

> Format a number for the number of decimal points.

> Format a cell for a percentage value.

> Use absolute cell references.

> Change the values in a SUM function.

> Use the IF function.

> Format the border around a group of cells.

ASSESSMENT POINT

Now let's assess the work. Look back at the table at the beginning of this section (**Target Point**) and decide on which of the statements you can answer 'Yes' to.

Did you do as well as you expected? Could you improve your work? Add a comment to your work to show what you could do to improve it so that next time you'll remember to do it the first time.

TASK BRIEF

The school drama department is producing a play and would like advice on managing the finances and deciding on what to charge for tickets, programmes and drinks.

PROJECT BRIEF

The school drama department has sent you an email with the following brief:

Project title:

Model of the drama department production.

We would like you to produce a spreadsheet model to assist us in our upcoming production so that we can break even or even make a small profit.

Important information about the production:

 The production will run for two nights.

 The costs involved are:

Hire of hall	£200.00
Printing of tickets	£25.00
Printing of programmes	£50.00
Costume hire	£500.00
Cost of refreshments	£100.00
Cleaning, etc.	£50.00

There will be 120 seats available on each evening, arranged as shown in the diagram below:

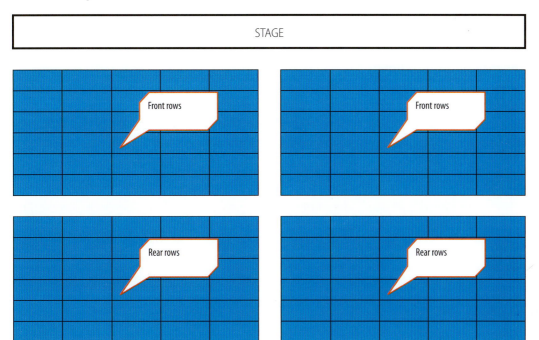

The cost of the front rows of seats should be higher than the rear rows.

 The audience will be encouraged to buy programmes and then drinks in the interval.

Project requirements:

We would like to use the model to:

 Experiment with different numbers of ticket sales as shown in the diagram below:

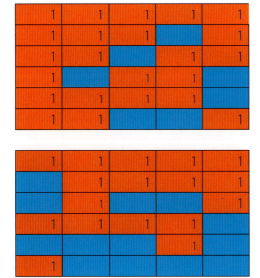
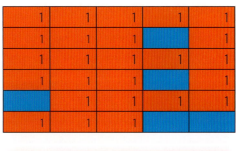
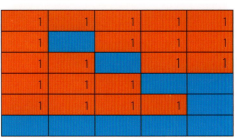

2   Try different ticket costs.

3   Experiment with different programme and drinks costs and the percentage of the audience expected to buy them.

The model should show:

1   The numbers of each type of seat sold on each evening.

2   The revenue from the ticket sales on each evening.

3   The number of programmes and drinks sold each evening and the revenue obtained from them, depending on the percentage of the audience expected to buy them.

4   The total revenue each evening.

5   The total revenue made over the **two** evenings.

6   The total revenue compared to the costs and whether there is a profit or a loss.

We would like a chart showing:

1   The revenue on each day.

2   The total revenue over the two days.

3   The profit or loss.

Your task now is to create this model.

You have all of the skills you'll need to build the model, now you have to demonstrate your capability and produce one for this particular purpose.

Level 3	Level 4	Level 5	Level 6
You have saved the file with a new name. You saved it as 'Project'	You have used 'Save As' to save the file with a new name, 'Project', in the correct folder	You have used an absolute cell reference	You have used the IF function
You have added simple formulas to find totals e.g. =A1+A2+A3	You have created a data table in a worksheet with details of different ticket prices and percentages of people buying programmes and drinks	You have used functions e.g. SUM	You have used formulas that use cell references from different worksheets
You have used the model to change variables e.g. ticket prices to try to make a profit	You have added new labels to the data sheet	You have used the model to investigate the percentage of people who will need to buy a programme and a drink and the prices you should charge for them	You have used the model to predict the revenue and profit or loss by changing ticket prices, programme and drink prices and percentages sold using sensible amounts
	You have formatted a cell to show percentages	You have created a chart to show the costs, revenue and profit or loss	
	You have used the model to investigate the number of tickets that should be sold to make a profit		

TARGET POINT

Have a look at the following statements before you start your project so you know what you are aiming for.

Level 7
You have developed the model independently and it shows the expected ticket sales, prices, percentages of programmes and drinks sold and their prices. It shows the total revenue expected and the profit or loss
You have used the model to investigate the target sales for tickets, programmes and drinks and their prices in order to make a profit

To meet this project brief you need to complete the spreadsheet model and chart, but that is only one part of the process that you would need to go through if you were creating these for a real business. The information below shows you how you could go about planning your documents. Use the target points to decide how you want to tackle it.

The Functional Skills listed below show you the skills you will be demonstrating in your work – but remember you have to know *why* you have chosen to demonstrate them in a particular way and how your choices match you audience and purpose for the documents.

> Organise the layout of your spreadsheet.

> Format the cells, text and numbers.

> Change the column widths.

> Use formulas and functions.

> Repeatedly fill cells with the same formula.

> Change variables.

> Create a chart.

> Test the spreadsheet.

This is quite a complicated model, so let's look at some ideas.

It would be a good idea to use four worksheets for this model:

> The first worksheet could be a data sheet where the costs, suggested prices and percentages of the audience buying programmes and drinks could be stored as shown in Figure Project.1.

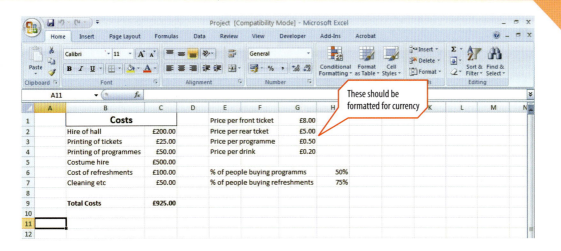

Figure Project.1

> There could then be two worksheets – one for each day, as the production lasts for two days. One of the sheets is shown in Figure Project.2.

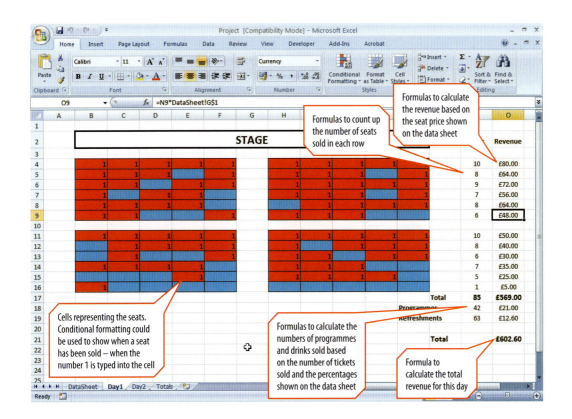

Figure Project.2

The fourth worksheet could be used to calculate the total revenue and work out the profit or loss. The chart could also be shown on this worksheet as shown in Figure Project.3.

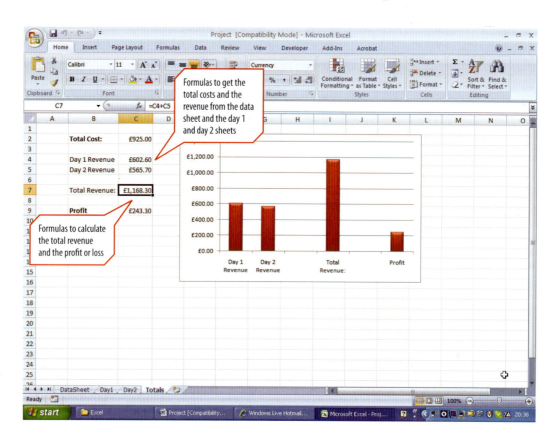

Figure Project.3

The drama department will then be able to change the variables on the data sheet:

- the price of front and rear tickets

- the price for programmes and drinks

- the percentages of the audience expected to buy programmes and drinks

- the seats expected to be sold on the day 1 and day 2 sheets.

As the drama department experiment with these variables, the revenue and profit or loss will change on all of the sheets because of the formulas used.

These are just some ideas you could use but you could design your worksheets completely differently as long as the model can be used to show:

- the numbers of each type of seat sold on each evening

- the revenue from the ticket sales on each evening

- the number of programmes and drinks sold each evening and the revenue obtained from them depending on the percentage of the audience expected to buy them

- the total revenue each evening

- the total revenue made over the **two** evenings

- the total revenue compared to the costs and whether there is a profit or a loss.

Now it's up to you. Good luck!

INDEX